FABULOUS Friendship Festival

Loving Wildly, Learning Deeply, Living Fully with Our Friends

BY SARK

Three Rivers Press
New York

SARK

copyright © 2007

All rights very reserved

Published in The United States By Three Rivers Press, an imprint of The Crown Publishing Group, a Division of Random House, Inc., New York.

www.crownpublishing.com

Three Rivers Press and The TUGBOAT Design are registered Trademarks of Random House, Inc.

Library of Congress Cataloging-in-Publication Data is Available Upon request.

ISBN 978-0-307-34169-3

Printed in SINGAPORE

SPECIAL Thanks to:

Carrie Thornton: Superb editor
Brandi Bowles: radiant Assistant
Mark McCauslin: cool production editor
Jennifer O'Connor: Delighted Designer
Jie Yang: Daring production person
Derek Gullino: Fabulous production person
Jean Lynch: Creative copy editing (any mistakes are all mine!)

10 9 8 7 6 5 4 3 2 1

First edition

THANKS TO THE WHOLE TEAM AT THREE RIVERS Press

Photo credit Kimberly wilkinson Page 154

Marvelous Assistance from you! Thank you.. "Hoogie" Marcy "The Dish" Marcy from Malcolm + special photographic help From Tvisha Donna, Carrie, Kathryn, Shannon & my ToTe FAM!

cultivating Delight © 2.001 on page 224

Cool cover input By Chris Tate Fabulous Additional cover consulting + lettering encouragement ChrisTate.com

permission granted By Diane Ackerman For Quote From her Book Cultivating Delight

S. Outstanding Cover Design S. Suzanne NASON TwistStudio.com

+ McNair wilson McNairwilson.com Thanks To The whole Gold Mirror City

THANKS to The Printers!

THIS BOOK IS
DEDICATED
WITH LOVE
TO MY DARLING SUSAN

TO:

Wonderfully From:

THIS BOOK
is
MY
GREAT BIG
Love note
to
Friends everywHere

THis includes YOU

I AM often astonished by the height and depth of friendships in my life. I've felt sheltered, nourished, supported and deeply cherished by my friends.

My gorgeous friendships have inspired me to write this book, and share the wonders, mysteries, frustrations and joys that friendships bring. I've compiled what I know and have learned, so that it can inspire and encourage you too.

we can inspire and encourage each other

Besides our families, our friendships are our foundations, diving boards and safe places to land.

This book is about deeply valuing those friendships. It's also about loving and learning from the friends you have, finding more if you need them, and learning how to be really great friends with your self. 7.

missy and me on the swingset

I remember my first best friend and can still cry when I think of how sweet our friendship was. We ate cream of tomato soup, built blanket forts, read the same picture books, and went on lake vacations together. We started out laughing on the swing set and stayed friends for many years. Our friendship showed me that I was loved outside of my family.

We are guided and strengthened by our friendships and we can use that strength to magnify and expand upon goodness in this world.

Our friendships are our real trust funds and will provide us and the world with too many miracles to count.

8.

Our close friends witness our triumphs, our growth and despair, our grieving and searching and most of all, our changes. Some friends are there for all of it, other friends travel along for shorter segments of the journey.

THIS BOOK is written like my journal, and includes my art and photographs, and places for you to add yours too. It is RICH and multilayered, just like our friendships are.

I've written about things you may have thought about friendships, but perhaps haven't said out loud. I'll ask you certain kinds of questions and provide space and channels for YOUR new thoughts about having friends and being a friend. I believe we must also PRACTICE being good friends with ourselves, and I will describe many new ways to do this.

we will share self-friendship revelations

THERE IS a whole world of friendship to consider: our history of friendship, friendship choices and styles, and who we are friends with today.

I'M GOING to write A lot in This BOOK About All The DimensioNs of FrieNdships — The Whole picture, not just The sunny smiles and Best aNGles. Those sunny smiles inspire us, But it's The Bleud of eAse and Difficulty THAT sustaiN us. I've Sometimes Felt **CHAlleNGed**, Discouraged or Alone when FrieNdships CHaNGe, FAde or eud For All sorts of reAsons. SiNce some of My FrieNdships Are My "FAMily of Choice," I've leArNed MaNy SigNificaNt lessons From The GrowTH aud The eudinGs of These KiNds of FrieNdships.

All of our FrieNdship experieNces provide us with perfect leArNiNG opportunities. I Think I've MADe Most of The MisTAkes you cau in FrieNdship, aud will write About These aud whAt I've leArNed.

since I continue to MAke misTAkes, There is no shortAGe of examples

I invite you to use This Book As A FrieNdship CelebrAtion Guide, eNerGizer aud FocusinG Device.

There Are THree parts to THis BOOK: CelebrAtions, CHAlleNGes, InteGration

10.

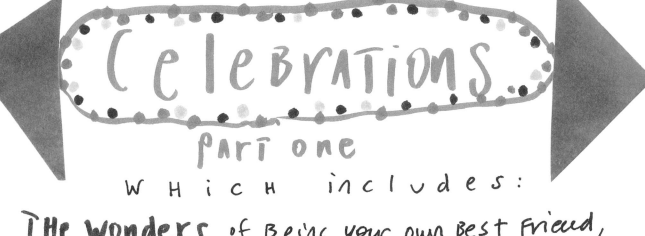

Celebrations...

Part one

WHICH includes:

THE Wonders of Being your own Best Friend, including A color-full wheel to Awaken and remind you About practicing This.

All The Kinds of Friends There Are, including imaginary friends and Books As Friends.

MAKING and creating new Friendships and How to DO THAT.

Friendships As "FAMily of choice" and WHAT That Means.

"Being A FABulous friend" Manifesto.

FABulous, Fresh Things to DO with Friends.

Great Questions to Ask and answer with close Friends.

ADventure itineraries to send yourself or Friends on.

New ways to ADMire and celebrate your Friendships.

Descriptions of eccentric Friendship GATHerings.

WAys to extravagantly lounge together.

CHALLENGES

PART TWO

WHICH includes:

- **Friendship** Difficulties, including Grudges and resentments and ways to release the
- **Jealous** feelings and what to do with these.
- **WAYS** to respond to negative friends.
- **WHEN** and why conflicts come and how to work with those energies.
- **Silences** in friendships and new perspectives about these.
- **Anger** and processes to move the energy.
- **Forgiveness**, including self-forgiveness: How, when and why.
- **MANAGING** time and energy in friendships and new ways to do it.

inteGRATioN

PART THREE

WHICH includes:

- THE BLENDING of celebrations and CHALLENGES creates our FABUlous friendships and WHAT THEy give to us.

- I've created A self-proclamation to remind us of THE splendors of our Friendships and How MuCH we Are tAUGHT, nourished and sustained By THem.

- THere is A section on "integration PRACTICE" and WHAT This is, and WAys to experience it.

13.

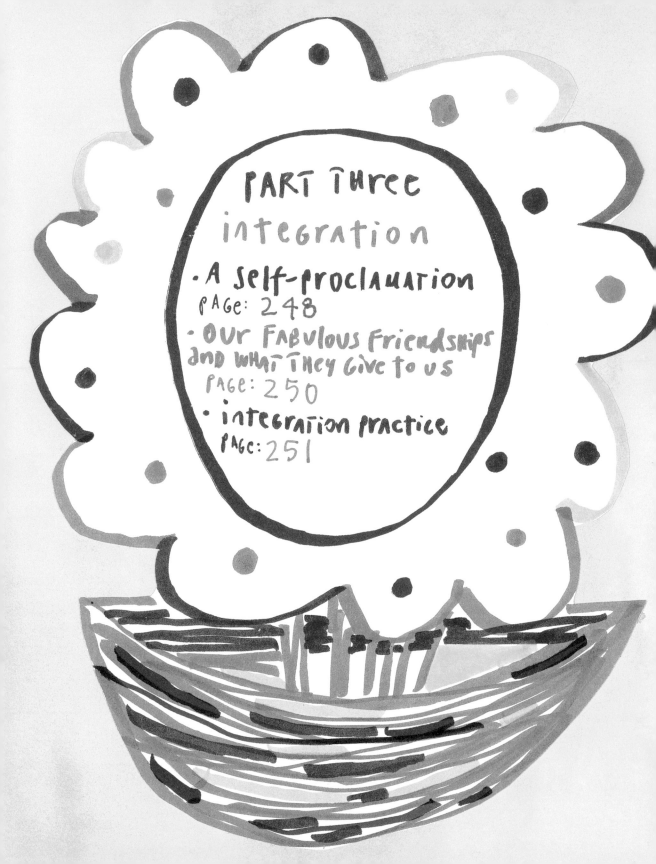

PART THree

integration

- A self-proclamation
- Our Fabulous Friendships and WHAT THEY Give to us
- integration practice

"Friendship with oneself is all-important, because without it, one cannot be friends with anyone else in the world"
Eleanor Roosevelt

CHAPTER ONE

SELF Friendship

"I have an inalienable, constitutional, and natural right to love whom I may, to love as long or as short a period as I can, to change that love everyday if I please" Victoria Wood Hull

Being your own Best friend

Being Best friends with yourself means that you've always there for the soul of friendship — which means consistently attending to your own emotional experiences, feelings, activities and all the "stuff" that life brings. It means that you Act for yourself first, "Filling your own well" Before going out to connect with others.

Friendship with yourself means that you maintain the relationship, no matter what else happens in your life. Many of us turn away from self-friendship when or if things feel difficult. We might feel or think that being friends with ourselves doesn't provide enough of what we need. It is easy to think that something outside of ourselves might be better, easier or more fun. Or, we might just feel tired of ourselves.

Self-friendship requires time and practice. This practice calls for us to be friendly with all the parts of ourselves we might consider ugly or unworthy.

Being "friendly with all the parts" doesn't mean you need to like it — you just need to feel it   21.

We were All Born with A Built-in "Best Friend:" ourselves. But most people Dont spend The necessary time learning How to truly nurture THAT Friendship. We often skip Doing The essential work THAT it TAkes to reAlly love our selves, and instead, Go out to Get From Friends WHAT we Think we need, or is Missing. DOING This essential work is CHALLENGING—it Can Feel scAry to see or experience our FlAws and FAILINGS, and Then continue to Apply unconditionAl love to ourselves. Also, This LACK of self-Friendship Can Multiply After years of self-neglect and ABandonment.

We MUST Listen closely To ourselves

BEING your own Best Friend means treating yourself As Kindly and respectfully As you Do your DeArest Friend.

I Most often want to quit Being Friends with Myself when I lAck The ABility to love Myself "No mAtter WHAT." For example, one of My FAMiliAr CHAllenges is intolerance, and it sHows up in My self-Friendship As impAtience or lAck of Acceptance when My "less Than ideAl" self sHows up.

Often we don't even recognize How to

give ourselves sweet, deep self-friendship, because
we're so busy **BUILDING A STRATEGY** to get
what we think we need in friendships with others.

Well let's see... if I call Her, THen sHe'll... THen
we can... and After THAT we'll.....

Looking outside yourself for friendship is

A lovely and splendid art in itself, but it is
subject to other people's time, availability,
and circumstances, which may or may not
match with you really need.

Being your own best friend means looking

inside your self for company, joy, commiseration,
fun, sympathy and endearing moments.

Here are some questions for you to ponder and answer.

WHAT kind of friend are you to your self?

DO you listen to your self attentively and with great compassion?

Are you liberally applying self-forgiveness?

DO you speak to and of yourself with kindness and respect?

Are you refusing to engage in negative self-talk
like blaming, judgment or self-criticism?

or, when you do, do you recognize it faster
and stop speaking in those ways?

23.

We often grant to other friends what we won't grant to our own self-friendship. We might be understanding with a friend the way we're not with ourselves. And, whatever we don't accept in a friend is usually what we don't accept in ourselves.

OH, SURE!
we'll shout
to a friend

We'll hear our friend speak about being overly busy or overwhelmed, and we supply suggestions, solutions or sympathy. We say things like:

"It's going to be okay. Can you take a rest or a break? Is there anyone that can help you, or can I help you?"

"I hear you! You're doing so much!"

Then, when it comes to ourselves, we're often ruthless and unforgiving, saying things like:

"I can't believe I didn't get it done, missed the appointment, forgot my friend's birthday or didn't check in on my sick friend. I'm never _____ . I'm always _____ ."

I've noticed that the words I speak to a dear friend are often shockingly different from the words I hear inside or speak to myself.

"I sustain myself with the love of friends" Maya Angelou

24.

I recommend writing down or speaking negative self-thoughts. This gets them out of your head and separate from you.

I FEEL SO ANGRY + HURT BECAUSE :
- I Forgot Bills BiRThDAY
- I didn't send my taxes on time
- any one didn't check on me when I was sick
- The Burner on my stove is Broken
- I'm sick of Always Being So sensitive

Get All
THE THOUGHTS
OUT THAT
Feel Hurtful
Sometimes I
Fill 6-10
PAGes !

write until you can't think of A single other negative thought, tiny or large

Then, CALL up on your "wise self" to answer each of the items on your negative list.

WISE VOICE GLADLY SPEAKS :
- Bill will love to Hear from you whenever you call
- Friends Don't keep score
- It's OK!, you can make mistakes. Find out what you need to do to correct it
- Give yourself the Attention you Are seeking from others
- you will get This Fixed - or not.
- your sensitivity is Beautiful and A Gift to This world

THIS wise self
Can Be Like an
internal COACH,
nurturing parent,
Higher self —
whatever works
Best for you As
A champion,
cheer leader and
positive supporter

25.

This new habit builds a basis of only speaking lovingly and kindly to yourself. Over time, you will be able to do this automatically, without thinking. You might also ask close friends to intervene if they hear you speaking unkindly about yourself.

Our close friends can remind us to be kind to ourselves

26.

Practicing self-friendship

> I intend to learn to CHOOSE to be great friends with my self each day

LIVING These words requires daily practice. My friendship with myself falters when there is a lack of awareness and self-care. If I'm not actively aware that I'm my own dearest friend, how can I treat myself as one? If I'm not caring for my self in nourishing, positive ways, my self-friendship will be limited to whatever I just happen to be able to do, or what was "left over" after being friends with everybody else.

.... of course we also receive by giving to our friends

I KNOW That some people worry that self-friendship sounds or seems selfish. When we hear about great friendships, and friendship kindnesses, we cheer and applaud, but if we are exquisitely kind and self-caring for ourselves, we think we need to do it quietly or furtively because it might be thought of as "too much" or selfish somehow.

"Alone and the soul emerges" walt whitman

27.

It is not selfish to love oneself.

A person can give so much to their friends that there is literally nothing left for them. This is where lonely despair and exhaustion can enter in.

despair enters in

I KNOW this despair, because when I wasn't actively being friends with myself, I looked outward all the time to receive nourishment from my friends. Then, if they were unavailable or busy, or we stopped being friends for some reason, it seemed that I had so much less.

I WAS MEASURING how I felt on the inside by what I thought I wasn't getting on the outside.

This is very common

Practicing being friends with ourselves means changing old habits into new ones. One of my practices is to write letters to myself, which I then re-read. Here's one of my reminder letters I wrote to myself:

"insist on yourself, never imitate." — Ralph Waldo Emerson

28.

DEAREST SUSAN,

Thank you for being such a good friend to yourself. I appreciate your friends with yourself. I appreciate your friendship and feel grateful for all the kindnesses you're showing to yourself. I love how you're going for daily long beach walks and eating sumptuous, nutritious food. Thank you for training such exquisite care of yourself.

Thank you for balancing work and play, and making sure you're getting enough play time. I can really tell you're more able to choose not to suffer, but instead deal directly with whatever hurts or stops you.

I thank you for telling your truth faster, and for paying close attention to your most alive choices, even when it feels uncomfortable to try new things.

I'm so glad you listen to yourself and to your friends. There is so much wisdom to share and reflect on. Thank you for spending plenty of time at home, meditating, creating and tea-drinking.

I love how you're choosing positive self-talk so much more, and how you value being friends with yourself more than being right, admired or pursued in some way.

I thank you for spending time on your self-friendship and for developing new ways to love you.

love, Susan

Practicing self-friendship means looking inside ourselves first, before deciding that something is lacking or missing from another friendship. If a friend has been unavailable or distant, ask yourself **How present and close you've been with your <u>self</u>** and then give that experience to yourself. From doing this practice, I no longer "blame" friends as often or automatically for whatever I used to think they weren't doing! I still sometimes struggle with the subject of initiating, and often keep track of how often I call first, or suggest something fun to do together. WHEN I BECOME AWARE THAT I'm doing this, I take it as **A SIGNAL** to tend to my own self-friendship and check to see if something is out of balance in my self-care.

Also, it seems clear that if I'm feeling happy in myself, it wouldn't matter who initiates

<u>I</u> often need reminders to:
STOP THINKING
and
Go outside
or

Go inside
and engage my body and mind through some type of movement and

BREATHING

Getting "out of my Head" connects me to my friendship with myself and reminds me of who I am at the essence level, and not just my personality.

These practices of meditation and movement are so simple, yet for years I didn't do them. I used to feel very disconnected and out of balance. This then meant that I attracted friendships that were disconnected and out of balance, and we all swirled in a toxic mixture together.

not fun!

I've Discovered that I can be a funny, loving, warm, intuitive and supportive friend to myself, and of course that means I can extend myself even more **Beautifully** to others.

Those friends then reflect that good energy back to me.

32.

rActicinG self-FrieNdshil
means THAT we can:

- ◎ Fully entertain and enjoy ourselves in Any circumstance or place
- ◎ Be our own witnesses to our Lives and dont need outside VALiDAtion
    offer specialized insights to ourselves
- ◎ Develop and strengthen our ABiLities to be our own Best Ally and protector
- ◎ Fill ourselves up with Good Things
- ◎ enjoy and feel Good with our own companionship

PrActice means THAT we Do it over and over, and sometimes Do it BADLy. Sometimes we'll forget How, why or Whether we want to be Friends with ourselves.

PrActice anyway

33.

I Asked My Friend Marney to write About Being Friends with Herself, and This is How She responded:

There is nothing simple About Being Friends with Myself. It's not About Giving Myself DAily pep TALKS, or leaving Myself love notes, or tAKing BuBBle BATHS on TvesDAys. It's ABout consciously creating relationships Between All The pArts of me THAT MAKE sense and MAKE me As whole and HAppy and TruThful to Myself As possible. THougH The MeTHoD can CHAnge often, I would sAy THAT The Most Crucial pArts of Being A compAssion Friend to Myself include:

- Asking Myself A lot of Questions so THAT I can Get to Know my preferences, interests and Beliefs Better every DAy
- surrounding Myself with wonderful people who support The true me
  ForGiving and learning From MisTAKes I HAve MADe, Am MAKing, or will MAKe
- Giving Myself A lot of Time for creating
- Gently working with Difficult memories and processes to Help me Become fuller and more truly me
- providing opportunities for connections Between All Aspects of Myself to Move towArd GreATer wholeness
- pAying Attention to Feelings, and when They Don't MAKe sense, Trying to notice Them But not Judge Them
- Giving My Heart lots of opportunities to love otHers in ActNG wAys THAT Feel Good
- embracing My nATurAl inclinations to Follow intuition, joy and synchronicity
- Accepting All THAT is imperfect About me
  MAKing plAns and supporting intentions THAT will MAKe me HeAlthier + HAppie
  HAving Fun, living Lightly and smoothly
MAKing A List Like This one so I Am in touch with whAT I Am Doing to Be A Good Friend to Myself

34.

Awakening and Feeding Self-Friendship

Center: Being Friends With Your Self ↓ pick a feeling or state of being explore it

Creative wedge:
- Make something new
- experience something creative
- invent something
- take a creative risk in some way

i Feel, i AM, creative
· Alive, energized, Abundant WHAT can you create?

Ordinary wedge:
- Let yourself feel ordinary without needing something else
- welcome your ordinary self
- Be willing to be seen as ordinary

i Feel, i AM, ordinary
"I'm okay. I'm Fine." It's a regular kind of time. everything is cool.

Angry wedge:
- let anger move
- express, explore
- let anger melt
- speak or write about anger
- Tell someone

i Feel, i AM, angry
"I'm mad"
"I feel furious, enraged"
"piss off"
"Grabby, discouraged"
"Just plain angry"

Wild:
i feel, i AM WILD
ZOOM
WHAT Have you never done & or Been Before? Go.

Play:
i Feel, i AM PLAY Full
Frisky Fun Juicy Jumping
What can you play? who can you play with? what does this Feeling want to go.

Happy:
i Feel, i AM HAPPY Joy-Full
I just feel so much Joy and happiness i AM so Blessed
· Make your joy visible
· Circulate it
· Magnify, multiply Joy
· let go and allow a new Feeling
· Share your Joy

Bored:
i Feel, i AM Bored
This is where self-friendship often flounders. "Bored" often covers up another feeling. explore your Boredom and see where it leads you.
· WHAT'S New right now?
· Who Can I Be While Bored?
· Write or speak about how Bored you Feel
· reach towards someone or yourself in a new way

Vulnerable:
i Feel, i AM Vulnerable fragile
· Allowing your vulnerability lets in strength.
· occupy your vulnerability by letting it just Be there.
Allow Vulnerability
· Sit quietly and Bless your vulnerable feeling
· speak or write about vulnerable experience
· Become aware that Feeling vulnerable is NOT weakness

Depressed:
i Feel, i AM Depressed
"I feel Dull, sad, low energy, crushed, folded, surrendered, depression."
· lie down right now
· Ask yourself "Do I need Allow Depression to shift, or not
· explore what feeling shows up next

Becoming and practicing being friends with ourselves means changing how we relate to who we are, and what we do. It means allowing how we feel. Many of us are not aware of how we're feeling or how to be with those feelings in self-nourishing ways

Self-Friendship resources

IMAGINE A WOMAN IN LOVE WITH HERSELF
PATRICIA LYNN REILLY

Quirkyalone
A Manifesto For Uncompromising ROMantics
SASHA CAGEN

A WALK on THE BEACH
Joan anderson

it's MY pleasure
MARIA RODALE and MAYA rodale

Grow
Lynne Franks

intimacy and solitude
STEPHANIE DOWRICK

True to Myself
ZiGGY Marley Song

WHen I LOVED Myself enough
KiM McMillen

"Friends are relatives you make for yourself"
Eustache Deschamps

Chapter Two

Kinds of Friends

"Animals are such agreeable friends— they ask no questions, they pass no criticisms"
George Eliot

Kinds of Friends

I'd like to honor and acknowledge all the types of friends there are. **I feel so very blessed** to have many kinds of friends in my life. I'm sure you do too.

- ## OLD FRIENDS.

  - **MY** friend MUGGY from 40 years ago just recontacted me and came for a visit. Among her many memories was that I was the only kid on the block whose mom bought her the **BiGGEST Box of Crayons.** (64 crayons Thanks Mom!)

  - **MY** friend KATHRYN from 30 years ago is still my good friend today. We're BOTH ARTISTS and talk about anything and everything in our lives.

  WHAT do you think keeps these kinds of connections strong through the years, or not? WHAT BREAKS these connections?

- ## instant friends.

  - **I JUST MET** a remarkable woman at eSalen in Big Sur. Her name is Gabriella, and we played the transformation game, soaked in the hot springs and swooned over Leonard Cohen music together.

39.

WHAT DO YOU THINK OPENS THE WAY FOR IMMEDIATE INTIMACY AND HOW DO YOU DECIDE WHETHER TO CONTINUE DEVELOPING A FRIENDSHIP?

neighbor friends.

- **MY neighbors** JIMMIE AND MARTI HAVE BECOME GOOD FRIENDS OF MINE, THANKS TO QUANTUM TALKS AT THEIR FRAME SHOP DOWN THE HILL.
- **MY neighbor** SALLY AND I SHARE A GARDEN VIEW AND APPRECIATION OF THE COURSE IN MIRACLES WORK. I ALSO ATTEND HER YEARLY 4TH OF JULY PARTY.
- **MY neighbor** MICHAEL AND I EXCHANGE WHIMSICAL NOTES IN OUR MAILBOXES.

WHAT NEIGHBOR FRIENDS DO YOU HAVE AND HOW WOULD YOU DESCRIBE THESE FRIENDSHIPS? WHY OR WHY DON'T YOU MAKE NEW NEIGHBOR FRIENDS?

animal friends.

- **MY CAT** JUPITER LIVED WITH ME FOR 17 YEARS AND BECOME A VERY DEAR FRIEND. WE COMMUNICATED TELEPATHICALLY, INTUITIVELY AND RECIPROCALLY.
- **MY DOG** FRIEND BRANDY LIVES IN CARMEL WITH PATRICIA AND I FEEL A UNIQUE FRIENDSHIP WITH HIM.
- **MY DOG** FRIEND CHARLIE LIVES IN AUSTRALIA WITH LEONIE AND HER PARTNER. WE'VE NEVER MET IN PERSON, BUT AS SOON AS I SAW HIS PHOTO, I KNEW WE WERE FRIENDS.

Are YOU FRIENDS WITH ANY ANIMALS? DO YOU BELIEVE THIS IS POSSIBLE OR FULFILLING?

in memory of Jupiter, A SUPERB CAT WHO WAS WITH ME FOR EVERY BOOK, AND NOW HAPPILY FLIES FREE FROM PHYSICAL REALMS

PHONE FRIENDS.

* ELISSA and I stay very close through numerous, often daily voicemail messages. The DEPTH and detail of these messages feels very supportive and is also in addition to seeing each other in person.

* KAREN and I exchange deeply encouraging voicemail messages, in addition to seeing each other.

WHAT is your experience of "phone friends?" Do you find these kinds of friendships to be VALUABLE? Why or why not?

EMAIL and online FRIENDS.

* MARNEY and I email delightfully about any subject, and built our friendship initially by phone and email.

I've hosted an internet community and message boards since 1998, and have formed hundreds of friendships through this medium. I've also personally met with many of my friends outside the message board community.

DO you have online or email friendships? Do you find this to be a viable or valuable way to form friendships? Why or why not?

SIBLING FRIENDSHIPS.

My brother Andrew and I have developed and maintained a friendship beyond the usual

41.

SiBLING relationship. It HAS involved
DOING emotionAL process work toGeTHer, trvTHe teLLING
And respect for eACH oTHer As ADULTs.

DO you HAve Any siBLING friendships? if
you Don't HAve Any siBLINGs, Do you iMAGine you
woULD or woULD Not Be friends?

Male/Female Friends.

My friend JOSHVA And I HAve BViLT A
Deeply intiMATE And enDeAring friendsHip.
THe FACT THAT He's A Man HAS Been rATHer
incidentAL.

My friend CLArk And I Are Good friends
And FreqVently Piscvss Communication style
Differences Between men And women, And GOOD TV.

DO you HAve friendships wiTH THe opposite
sex? How Are THey Different From oTHer friendships?

Couple friends.

Wes And JUDy And I Are GreAT friends,
And I'm friends wiTH eACH of THem sepArAtely
Also. I'm inspired By THem As A couple.

VAL And CLArk And I Are very close friends,
And I Also Appreciate And ADMire THem As A
couple.

DO you HAve "couple" friendsHips? How Do you
experience THis type of friendship?

42.

Former lover friendships.

- MCNAIR and I are friends now after spending 5 years in a romantic relationship. We both participated in a "relationship Autopsy" to bring closure to that and then begin a friendship.

  Are you friends with any former lovers? Why or why not?

ELDER Friendships.

- **All** My life, I have had friendships with people considerably older than me. I've greatly benefited from their wisdom and mentoring, and from their mistakes.

  AT 10, My best friend Mr. BOGGS, was 80
  AT 30, My friend MIRIAM was 90
  AT 35, My friend ISABEL was 80

  I've just made a new friend named KAY, who is 78. I also have a number of good friends who are a decade or more, older than me.

  Do you have any elder friendships? Why or why not?

I Think it's important to <u>recognize</u> and <u>celebrate</u> all the different kinds of friends in our lives!

BOOKS AS Friends

BOOKS Are Like Doors to other worlds, and My Friendship with Myself Has Grown immeasurably Because of Those Doors. **I open** the cover of A BOOK, step inside and Am often transformed in some way, and continue Growing long After. **Some of My FAvorite Friendships** HAve Been Described in BOOKS. I've learned to be A Better Friend By WHAT I've reAD.

EARTHLY PARADISE BY Colette • AWAKened My self-Friendship

My FAMILY And oTher Animals BY Gerald Durrell • portrayed WHAT it "sounds" Like to Be Friends with your FAMILY

I Know WHy The CAGed Bird Sings By MAYA Angelou • showed me How and WHy to Be Friends with LIFE

TrACKS BY roByn DAvidson • revealed TruTHs About Being Friends with Animals

44.

AS companions, books are steadfast—
Always willing to spend time with me.

AS conversationalists, books are largely
unequaled and our dialogue is DEEP
and often unmatched for originality.

BOOKS keep watch as I sleep, and are
here when I wake up.

BOOKS gather in

CLUMPS

and STACKS

and corners, and
they live inside bookstores and libraries,
where I go to visit them.

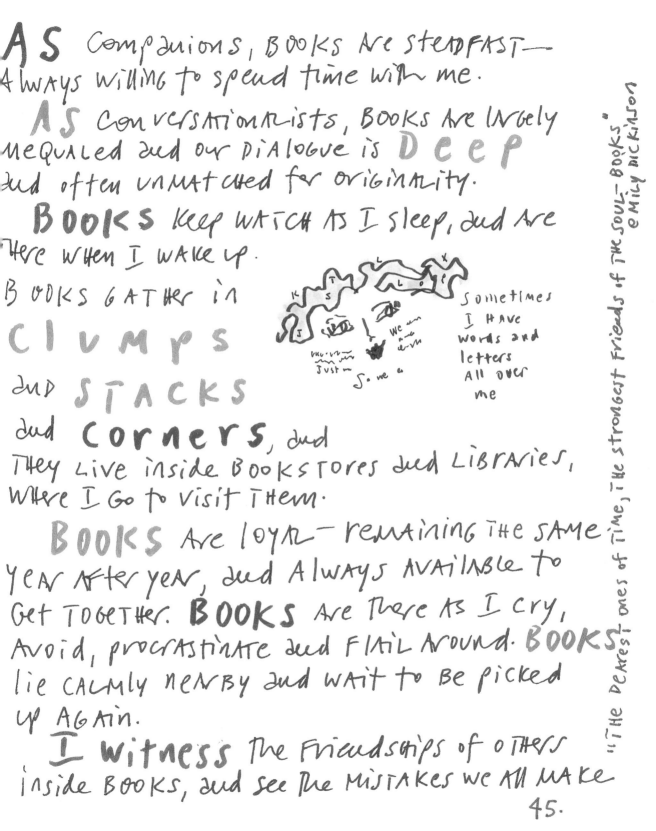

Sometimes
I have
words and
letters
all over
me

BOOKS are loyal—remaining the same
year after year, and always available to
get together. BOOKS are there as I cry,
avoid, procrastinate and flail around. BOOKS
lie calmly nearby and wait to be picked
up again.

I witness the friendships of others
inside books, and see the mistakes we all make

45.

"The dearest ones of time, the strongest friends of the soul—books"
@ Emily Dickinson

As we love, communicate and FIGHT with each OTHer.

I GIVE BOOKS as GIFTs to my Friends, and we are Forever connected By THe words and experiences we sHare As A result of

reading THe SAME BOOKS

I MUST COUNT BOOKS as some of My truest Friends, and AM GrAteFUL To THe writers and CreATors of THose BOOKS, WHo Are My "virtuaL Friends" As A result.

THank you To THe writers and THe reaDers I AM So GrAteFULL

"THe love of learning, THe sequestered nooks, and ALL THe sweet serenity of Books"
Henry wordsworTH LongFellow

IMAGINARY FRIENDS,
or FrIeNDS I WISH I HAD,

I WISH I HAD A little "POCKET FrIend"
THAT COULD GO everyWHere with me.
I WOULD TAKE OUT THIS MiniATure
Friend WHenever I needed COMPANY.
THere WOULD Be lots of **GIGGLING**
and secret tellinG.

dear
little
POCKeT
Friend

THe POCKeT FrIend WOULD HAVE
A tiny voice

I WISH I'd HAD FriendsHips with
Gertrude stein and Colette in 1920s PAris.
I'd HAVE SMOKed THose MiniATure CiGArs and
we'd HAVe stAyed up late, WeArinG VeLVeT,
DIScussinG literAture and ArGuinG too.

I WISH I'd HAD A Friendship with MATisse
and THAT Hed DOne A pAintinG of me.

I WISH I'd Been Friends with PippiLongstocking
and THAT we'd HAD topsy-turvy crooked Houses
next DOor to eACH oTHer.   47.

I WISH I WAS FRIENDS WITH MAYA Angelou MORE THAN I AM NOW. SHE INVITED ME FOR FRIED CHICKEN AND I FELT TOO SHY TO ACCEPT.

I WISH I'd BEEN FRIENDS ENOUGH WITH KATHARINE HEPBURN TO HAVE PLAYED PARCHEESI WITH HER.

I WISH I HAD A FRIEND NOW WHO WOULD HOLD SALONS EACH MONTH IN HER ECCENTRIC MANSION IN SAN FRANCISCO. THERE WOULD BE FASCINATING PEOPLE THERE AND BEGUILING WOMEN AND MEN.

I WISH MY PHYSICAL WORLD FRIENDSHIP WITH MY CAT JUPITER COULD HAVE GONE ON ALL OF MY LIFE.

I WISH I HAD A FRIENDSHIP ORGANIZER WHO WOULD CREATE AN IDEAL SCHEDULE TO SEE AND SPEND TIME WITH ALL OF THE MAGNIFICENT FRIENDS I HAVE NOW.

SCHEDULE WINDOWS
OPPORTUNITIES TO BE WITH FRIENDS

WHO WOULD your IMAGINARY FRIENDS BE?

WHO WOULD you LIKE TO BE FRIENDS WITH?

48.

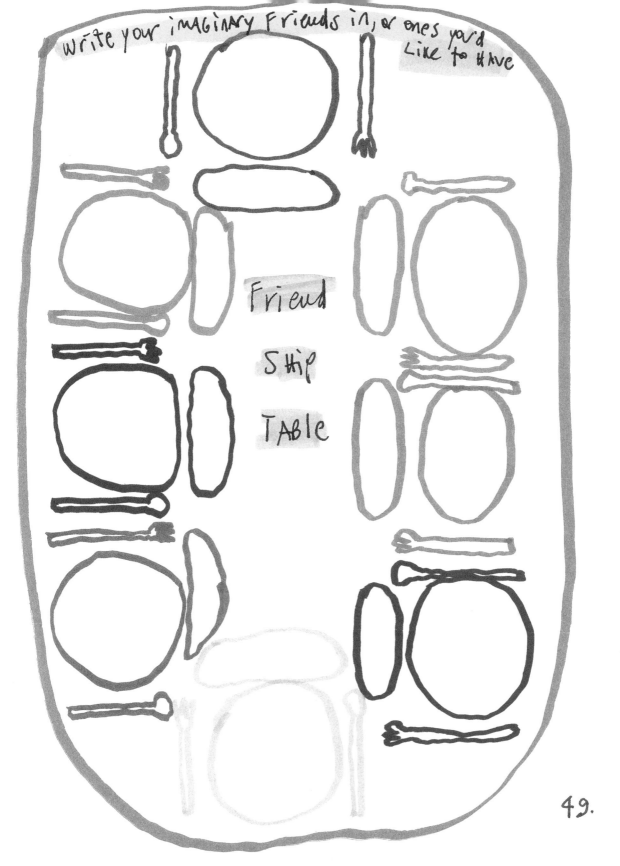

write your imaginary friends in, or ones you'd Like to Have

Friend
Ship
TABle

49.

Being Friends With A Child

I HAVE A FRIEND NAMED JONAH, AND HE'S 2½ YEARS OLD. HE'S SHORT IN SIZE, AND LONG IN LOVE. aDORABLE little Button of A Boy

ALTHOUGH JONAH IS A CHILD, I CONNECT TO HIM ON A SOUL LEVEL, AND SOUL LEVELS HAVE NO CHRONOLOGICAL AGE. All I KNOW IS THAT I FEEL JONAH'S FRIENDSHIP, AND SPEND MORE TIME WITH HIM BECAUSE OF IT.

People OFTEN ASSOCIATE BABYSITTING AS THE ONLY WAY TO SPEND TIME WITH YOUNG CHILDREN, AND I KNOW WITH CERTAIN TYPES OF KIDS THAT'S TRUE.

I experience My time with JONAH Differently.

Recently I SPENT THE AFTERNOON WITH JONAH. HIS MOM WAS WORKING, AND HIS DAD WAS AWAY ON A TRIP. WE PACKED OUR BACKPACKS WITH SNACKS AND DIApERS AND THE SIppy CUP, AND GOT DRESSED AND WENT OUT.

50.

By the time I got him into his car seat, I felt a bit tired and also a little giddy at the prospect of Adventures out in the world with my friend JONAH.

I Asked if He wanted to go to the Beach, and He smiled and calmly said, "Yes." We walked together towards the water, and all of a sudden, He stopped and pointed.

A group of young girls were gathered

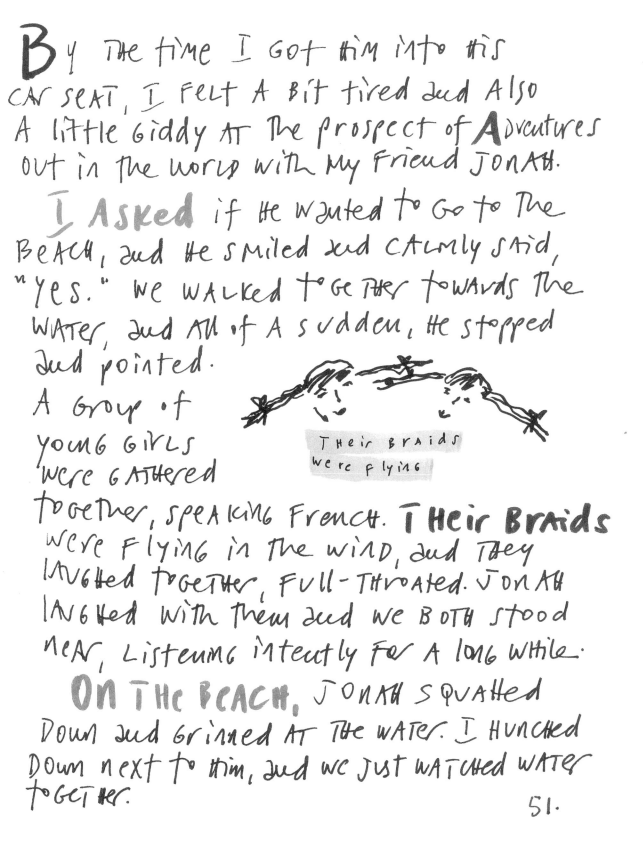

Their braids were flying

together, speaking French. Their Braids were flying in the wind, and they laughed together, Full-throated. Jonah laughed with them and we both stood near, Listening intently For a long while.

On The Beach, Jonah squatted down and grinned at the water. I hunched down next to Him, and we just watched water together.

LATER we visited the bookstore, the pet store, and then my house, where we invented games to play together and laughed uproariously. **THAT DAY,** I felt very aware of how much I value Jonah as a friend. Almost everything we did and experienced together, were things I would do with a friend.

Of course there are special considerations in our friendship. Jonah is an exuberantly alive 2½ year old, and I have no interest in him acting like a "little adult." Also, when we're together, he is in my care as a child, and I take that as a primary and sacred responsibility. But apart from the age differences and the roles we occupy, at the essence level, I consider him to be my friend.

I THINK there is great value in adults being friends with children. I think they need witnesses to their lives that are not only other parents or other kids.

"COME AWAY, OH HUMAN CHILD! TO THE WATERS AND THE WILD"   W.B. YEATS

I HAVE OTHER friends THAT HAPPEN to BE children, and Deeply VAlue This in My Life.

I encourAGe You to consider children in your Life As friends too. Here's a space to List THem, and include photographs too.

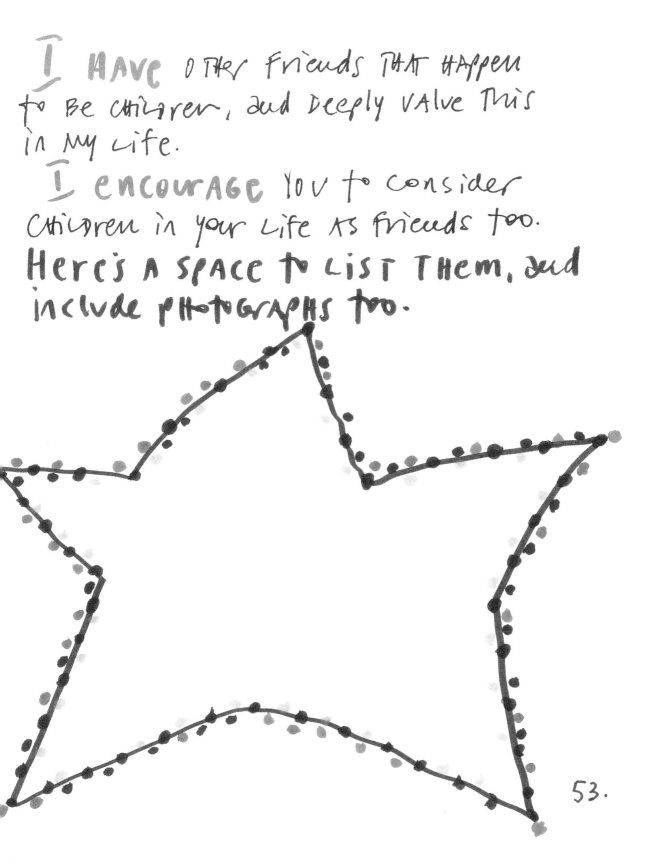

Kinds of friends resources

Between Friends
MFK Fisher and me
Jeannette Ferrary

Henry Miller's Book of Friends
Henry Miller

From May Sarton's well
Selection and photographs edith royce schade

planetSARK.com
"The Marvelous Message Board"

Artella wordsandART.com
an extravaganza of fun, resources and creative community

The inspiration phone line by SARK
415 546 3742

HowMuchJoy.com
Bursting with Joy

The True story of Owen & Mzee
A remarkable Friendship
isabella hatkoff
craig hatkoff
peter greste
paula kahumbu

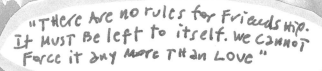

"There Are no rules for Friendship.
It must Be left to itself. We cannot
Force it any more Than Love"

William Hazlitt

Chapter Three

Making and Creating New Friendships

"Friendship is Born At That moment
When one person says To another,
'What! You too? I Thought I Was The
only one'

C. S. Lewis

Butterfly
Sky
of
Friends

© SARK '07

WAYS TO MAKE AND BE FRIENDS

I remember THAT SONG; "MAKE NEW Friends, BUT KEEP THE OLD, ONE is SILVER AND THE OTHER GOLD." THAT SONG DIDN'T EXPLAIN HOW TO **MAKE** NEW FRIENDS. I ALSO REMEMBER MY MOTHER TELLING ME THAT IT WOULD BE HARDER TO MAKE FRIENDS AS I GOT OLDER AND WASN'T IN SCHOOL ANYMORE.

MOMS SHARE THEIR EXPERIENCE OF LIFE

recently, I WENT TO AN EXPERIENTIAL LEARNING CENTER IN CANADA. I CHOSE NOT TO TAKE A CLASS, BUT JUST TO TAKE A VACATION. THIS MEANT THAT MOST OF THE PEOPLE THERE MADE FRIENDS THROUGH THEIR CLASSES, AND ON THE FIRST DAY, I SAT IN THE DINING ROOM ALONE, WISHING THAT I HAD A FRIEND.

I FELT VERY SHY AND OUT OF PLACE, AND ABSOLUTELY UNABLE TO "REACH OUT" AND MAKE A FRIEND. I REMEMBER FEELING PARALYZED AS A TEENAGER IN THE SCHOOL CAFETERIA, CLUTCHING

lonely SUSAN

My food tray and looking **WILDLY** around for friendly faces to sit with. Often I ate alone, wishing I HAD A Friend.

So Here I was at age 51, feeling some of the same feelings. Just then, a man walked over with his food tray and said,

"Mind if I join you?"

I immediately exclaimed:
"I'm going to copy you!" He smiled and asked what I meant. I said,

"I've Been wishing I HAD A Friend Here, and just **LOVE** How simple you MADE it, just asking if you could join me."

We HAD A lovely TALK ABout spontaneous Friendships, and what it takes to MAKE Friends.

I left the Dining room in good spirits, and **SKiPPed** Down the path to my cabin. On my way, I spotted A WOMAN CARRYING BOOKS on the ADJACENT PATH. I CALLed out A **good evening** to Her, and we began talking.

"Friendships Are Discovered rather Than MADE" HArriet Beecher Stowe 58.

Her name was Carol, she was about my age, there by herself, and also on vacation. We made a plan to have dinner together, and over the days I spent with Carol, we went on l o n g beach walks, ate homemade ice cream, built a bonfire, and went kayaking at night through bioluminescent waters. We also talked about _it's like stars in the water_ the deaths of our parents, laughed about all of our faults, and read to each other from books. By the end of our time, Carol and I had become such close friends that we cried when we said goodbye.

Carol left this poem for me from the book she was reading:

"Something opens our wings,
Something makes boredom and hurt disappear
Some one fills the cup in front of us,
We taste only sacredness"
— Robert Bly from Anam Cara
By John O'Donohue

This kind of "vacation friendship" sprang out of unusual experiences. So how do we make new friends during our "ordinary lives?"

59.

1. Be on The lookout Fr someone
THAT just looks like your Friend
THE OTHER DAY I WAS WALKING on THE BEACH,
and SAW A WOMAN with striped socks and
A curious HAT. I immediately THOUGHT THAT
SHe looked like My Friend.

cute striped socks

i cannot DRAW THE
HAT it WAS So curious

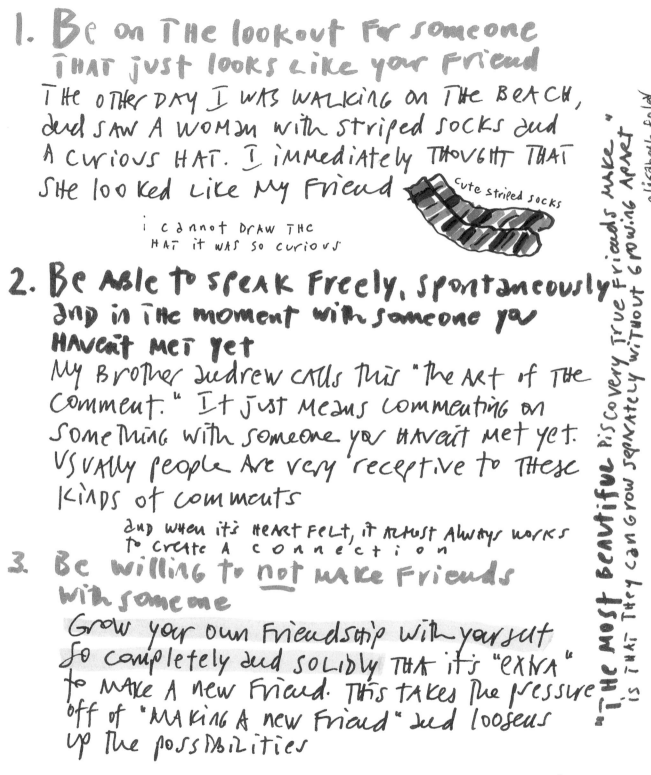

2. Be Able to speak Freely, spontaneously
and in The moment with someone you
HAVen't MET yet
My Brother Andrew calls this "the Art of THE
Comment." It just Means commenting on
Something with someone you HAVen't met yet.
USUALLY people Are very receptive to THese
Kinds of comments

and when its HEARt FeLt, it Almost Always works
to create A c o n n e c t i o n

3. Be willing to not make Friends
with someone
Grow your own Friendship with yourself
So completely and SOLIDLY THAT it's "EXTRA"
to MAKE A new Friend. This takes The pressure
off of "MAKING A new Friend" and loosens
up The possibilities

"THE Most BEAUTIFUL Discovery True Friends make
is THAT They can grow separately without Growing APART"
– elizabeth foley

60.

I ASKED THE WOMAN ON THE BEACH WITH STRIPED SOCKS if SHE KNEW WHY SO MANY STARFISH HAD WASHED UP

We BEGAN WALKING and TALKING ABOUT GARDENS, literature, Avoiding work and How annoying people can Be sometimes. At one point, we SAT on the pier In THE TWILIGHT, and SEA lions popped up, BreATHING AUDIBLY AS THOUGH THey were "listening" to Us. In our Discussion of literATure, BOOKS were Mentioned — My BOOKS, and I ASKed if SHe HAD reAD THEM.

She didn't know I WAS SARK

She Blurted out — "I've tried to reAD THAT WOMAN! I can't seem to, But I Give Her BOOKS AwAy to Friends."

I couldn't resist AsKing Her WHy SHe couldn't reAD THEM.

"THey Are Just too MUCH 'treAT yourself' and Im From New Jersey." SHe ADDed, LAUGHing; And you know we don't 'treAT ourselves' in New Jersey." We lAUGHed ABout This, and then I SAid to My new Friend, "This is Kind of AwKwArd, But I HAve to tell you THAT Im

61.

"THAT WOMAN" who wrote those books.
She just stared at me.

"Oh. My. God. Shit!"

We laughed and continued talking.
I'm not sure if we'll meet again — not
because of her comment — but because we're
both kind of **loners** and **non-planners**.
Perhaps we'll meet serendipitously again.

I think that making and creating new friends
can happen because of:

- **Opportunity:** Being in places where other people
are, and creating an opportunity to communicate.

- **Willingness:** Being willing to reach out in
some way to another person.

- **Allowing:** Allowing yourself the gifts of
spontaneous expression with other people.

- **Finding:** Finding connecting points between
yourself and another.

- **interest + Desire:** Declaring your interest and
desire, and this will actually create opportunity.

- **Humor:** it's funny being human, and we
can share those funny moments with other people.

Outside of dining rooms, I usually make and create new friends easily, and am blessed by the variety of friends in my life

so blessed

Of course, there are differences between MAKING friends and KEEPING friends, and I'm still learning about the communication arts it takes to keep friends.

and let them go

I believe that making new friends is also related to feeling WORTHY, interesting and inspiring. I also think it's important to realize that all of us feel "less than" sometimes, and to remember that we are

ENOUGH

Even when we feel less than interesting, inspiring or "worthy." We all want REAL friends to relate to and with, not some idealized version of the person or ourselves.

Our faults and flaws are in all of our friendships, and contain important gifts and lessons.

63.

Ways to Find out About A Friend and yourself in the Friendship.

especially A new Friend

Each Friendship Benefits From A **"NAVIGATION period."** It's Good to Find out From A Friend During This time:

- **W**HAT Their Definitions of Friendship Boundaries and limits Are, and yours too

- **H**ow They can support or not support you, and How you can Do The same?

- **A**re They truthful? Are you? Also WHAT level of TRUTH?

- **D**o They Like The "real" you, Are you Able to SHOW THAT to eAch oTHer?

Some of THIs will Be Discovered orGanically During your friendship, But it can Also Be Good to HAVE A Discussion About your pArticulAr friendship styles and HAbits in The BeGinning and see WHAT This friendship is offering to BOTH of you.

"Wishing to Be Friends is Quick, But friendship is slow-ripening fruit" Aristotle

64.

Friends as "Family of Choice"

I remember smiling when I first heard the phrase, "Family of Choice." The whole concept that our family of origin is one thing, and we can choose other alternative families in friendships to support us, seemed like an incredible solution due to my own lack of family support.

At that time, I didn't realize that my psychological makeup would lead me to recreate my family of origin in whatever friends I "picked" as my family of choice.

So, I duplicated my domineering mother, abandoning father, and abusive older brother in the friends I chose. I also experienced my unconditionally loving mother, endearing father and supportive brother through other friendship

CHOICES I MADE. UNTIL I worked Through These **re creation** PAtterns in TherApy and self-HEALING, I continued to recreate my fAmily of origin. untiL Then, The whole concept of ActuAlly choosing FrieNds who could Act As FAmily, FeLt Murky to me.

It seemed

All kinds of Friends Appeared

Like I just found or met Friends According to circumstances or serendipity, and then just "MADE DO" with whoever They were.

For exAMple, I wAs used to ADApting to BAD and inAppropriAte BeHAvior, so I chose DrAmAtic and wildly inAppropriAte Friends to mAtch my ADAptAtion.

MY FAther wAs A trAveLing sAlesMan who WAS rArely Home, so Before I worked Through my pAttern, I "CHOSE" pArtners who Lived elsewhere and cAme to visit infrequently.

MY FATHER'S ABSENCES promoted an abandonment awareness in me that caused me to sometimes experience distance as being abandoned. I often "ASSIGN MEANING" to friend's absences. THAT meaning is almost never factual or representative of How A friend truly feels.

I Frequently

super THICK STURDY HEART

Discover THAT A Friend missed me just as much as I missed them.

I've now learned to check in, to ask about hidden meanings, to explore with friends what something means to them. In these ways, we can effectively challenge previous patterns, and develop healthier families of choice.

I often felt lonely and isolated in my family of origin, so it's been important to me to GATHER MY TRIBE, My community. and keep them close.

67.

One time, my MOTHer was visiting and witnessed the closeness Between me and My Friends. She exclaimed:

"WHY do you TALK with your Friends so MUCH? WHy Don't you All just Grow up?"

she Just didn't understand The intimacy

I Assured Her THAT we were "Growing up" in FUNdAMENTAL new WAYs, and THAT our communications supported This.

There WAS VALue For me in the independence I WAS TAUGHT and Conditioned to; However, I Wanted to learn More About interdependence — WHere the support is Mutually Created.

I Began exploring This subject with All of My Friends, About support and How it Feels to Be supported. We're Discussing interdependence and Mutual support As well.

During one of these discussions, my friend Larry once said to me:

"Sometimes my support just won't feel COMFORTABLE."

This was a new concept for me. In my family of origin, I'd mostly experienced minimal support, or no support. In my family of choice, I'd experienced a kind of "remothering" or all-encompassing support, where friends spoke from a kind of "script" I'd given them. This kind of support felt nurturing, entirely positive, and very warm.
Also, at times, Artificial

Larry's kind of support sometimes felt CHALLENGING or upsetting to the me that wanted comfort and ease, and the script! Yet I often trusted Larry in his observations and experiences with me. So Larry has said the unpopular things, given me FEEDBACK

69.

THAT'S FELT pAinfUL, aud offered support
in profound wAys.

I THink THAT our Friends Are our
"Life Teachers," aud truly, FAMilies
of Choice Are THAT For eACH OTHer, if
consciously chosen aud Applied.
and THere is no script on Guidelines

I FeeL so excited to HAve expanded
My FAMily THrov6H Choosing My Friends.
It's Like tAking All THe 600D From
My FAMily of ori6in, aud MVLtipLying it.

I HAve experiences now of
vnconDitiomar Love and support
THAT I WAS seeking in My FAMily of
ori6in, THAT I THOVGHT I'd never FinD.

70.

My friends are now my Tribe,
my **FAMILY**, my **Mirrors**.

I am now the family member
that I wish I'd had growing up, and
I'm continuing to "Grow up" in these new,
conscious chosen ways.

MY choice of myself as my
own family is primary to my growth.

Once you make a new friend,
or for friends you already have,
you can write a "Manifesto" or use
the one I've written in the next pages.

THIS celebrates and defines
that connection, and helps your
friendships grow even more

FABULOUSLY.

Being A FABULOUS Friend

To ourselves and others
A Manifesto

Through fierce and feeble, power-full and pathetic times, we open our hearts to each other completely

When there is anger, we trust in our capacity to hold it, and adjust our velocity of expression of anger to be respectful. We grow through conflict, and learn to lift each other up

Through spirit, we provide a wide and deep resting place for each other. We challenge each other gently and firmly when necessary

In joy & pleasure we dedicate our energy and time

We are teachers for each other, and use a wide-angle lens for seeing love

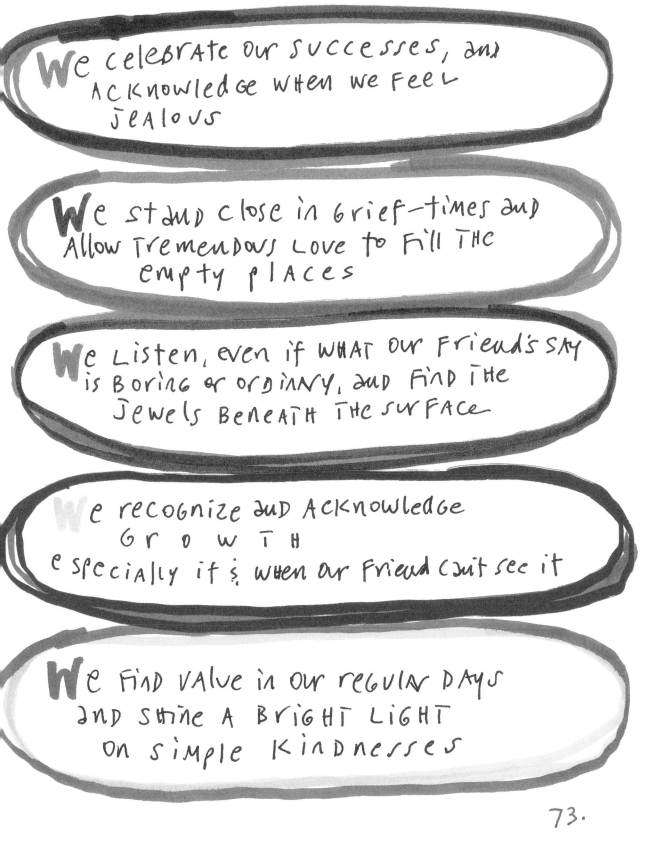

We celebrate our successes, and
Acknowledge when we feel
jealous

We stand close in grief-times and
Allow tremendous love to fill the
empty places

We listen, even if what our friend's say
is boring or ordinary, and find the
jewels beneath the surface

We recognize and acknowledge
GROWTH
especially if & when our friend can't see it

We find value in our regular days
and shine a bright light
on simple kindnesses

73.

We work with our own qualities and tendencies, and heal wounds that would otherwise be projected onto a friend
when we do practice projection, we consciously realize it

We tell the truth faster, even if it's painful or difficult
we forgive ourselves when we're not able to do this

We see clearly beyond false impressions and forced smiles, and other disguises that prevent us from witnessing the essence of a friend

We hold our friendship in sacred holy space, especially through humor, lightness and exploration

We listen and speak with our whole hearts whenever possible

We forgive continuously our friends and our own friendship flaws

We collect and display gratitude and share moments of beauty with our friends

We multiply our friends with age and time, to forever, to infinity

We love truly, our dear friends our ever-growing friendships, and honor completely the friendship with ourselves

75.

MAKING and CREATING NEW FRIENDSHIPS resources

TRUTH and BEAUTY: A Friendship
Ann Patchett

Into the Tangle of Friendship
Beth Kephart

Boundary issues
Jane Adams Ph.D.

Playing the Quantum Field
Brenda Anderson

A Weekend to Change your Life
Joan Anderson

Benevolentplanet.com
Connect with new friends in *The Compassion-Fruit Group *co-sponsored by Artella

Comfortqueen.com
Meet new Friends in matters of relationships, health and spirit

Living Artfully
Create the Life you imagine
Sandra Magsamen

How friends LIFT us up

After my mother died, I MARCHED through all the tasks and details surrounding her death, like a good little perfectionist.

Then I came home and fell completely apart.

This "falling apart" took the shape of a plot I hatched to take my car and my cat and drive to Kansas and live anonymously there for the rest of my life.

I decided that it hurt too much to love or be loved, and that a "big escape" was the best solution.

~ i wasn't thinking very clearly —

For part of a day, I packed and ignored voicemail messages. I knew they were all from friends asking how I was, and I didn't want my friends to know how desperate I'd become. LATER that day, I heard my friend Larry outside my door saying cheerfully:

79.

"SOMETHING HAS JUST BEEN DELIVERED FOR YOU! I'll JUST leAVE iT outside your DOOR."

I OPENED THE DOOR lATER TO COLLECT WHATEVER WAS THERE, And SAW A BiG GLEAMING POT, SURROUNDED BY VEGETABLES And A BiG BOUQUET of SUNFLOWERS.

I THEN REMEMBERED THAT My FRIEND ELISSA HAD SAID SHE WAS MAKING ME CHICKEN SOUP.

i JUST SIGHED AT THE BEAUTY

Thank you to MY DEAR ELISSA

THEN MY DOORBELL RANG.

IT WAS My FRIEND VAL. "I know I don't USUALLY JUST DROP OVER, BUT I FELT COMPELLED TO visit And ASK you TO COME WITH me TO A BEAUTIFUL SPOT. you can keep your PAJAMAS on"

So of course I did

WE DROVE TO A new place neAr My HOME CALLED THE WARMING HUT, lOCATED ON A WONDERFUL STRETCH OF BEACH neAr THE GOLDEN GATE BRIDGE.

80.

I SAT on the seawall, ocean spray splashing my feet, watching seagulls and children CAVORT in the water. I ate a roasted vegetable sandwich and felt a smile beginning.

THEN it was time to go, and Val drove me back home. I felt depressed as soon as I stepped out of her car, and then realized I could just go back to that seawall, so I did.

I CALLED every friend I have in San Francisco, and told them I'd be sitting there all day and to come and visit me.

ALL DAY I SAT and laughed with dear friends, and just soaked in the love, and felt pieces of my soul KNIT TOGETHER WHEN I ~~██████████~~ The Best Kind of Knitting returned home to the splendor of the homemade soup, I just wanted to admire it. Somehow I couldn't eat it. Then I felt embarrassed to admit this to my friend Elissa.

81.

I Finally told Her the truth.

"You know I rarely eat chicken, and this soup was such a symbol of love and redemption for me, I simply couldn't eat it. I know it was a lot of work and it's hard to explain, but I just HAD to keep it Here Without consuming it. Can you possibly understand?"

She DiD understand, and we HAD a long talk about the "Symbolic soup" and what it HAD Done for me, without my even eating it!

For so many years my friends have Been Lifting me Up, Attending to my moods and Dreams and Broken places. They've Been standing Beside me in Celebration and JOY, Applauding my Growth and Discoveries, Listening to me when All is Dark.

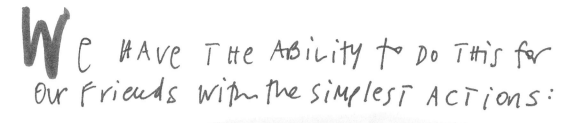

We have the ability to do this for our friends with the simplest actions:

- By listening deep
- By looking into our hearts
- By being there

Our friends can **swoop in** and attach wings to us, or sit quietly nearby as we pack our bags. Our friends **lift** us up and we can do the same for them.

ATTACHING WINGS TO A TRAVELING Friend

83.

Giving and Receiving in Friendships

"Friends Don't Keep score"

This is a lovely and prescriptive statement and most of us don't follow it. Most of us DO "keep score," usually silently. Some of this behavior is helpful, because a friendship needs to be **reciprocal,** and by maintaining some kind of awareness of who gives and who receives, reciprocal balance in our friendships occurs.

In the act of giving and receiving, I believe that most of us are far more comfortable and experienced in **Giving** to friends.

We give our **Time,** our **skills,** our **Advice, ideas** and **energy. Most** of us do this eagerly and willingly with no conscious thoughts of balance or reciprocity.

This willingness to give can change if or when the reciprocal balance is not maintained. I experienced this recently with a friend, where I had initiated a certain favor and activity over a long period of time.   i frequently made breakfast for us

Then my friend extended that same activity and favor to another friend.
     He began cooking for other friends and not me!

When I heard about this, I reacted by mentally counting all the times I had "given" and feeling how unfair it seemed.

I finally told my friend how I'd been feeling. I felt needy, pathetic and petty as I detailed my feelings.
My friend listened intently and said:

"I totally understand what you're saying and would probably feel the same way. Thank you for being brave and discussing it. Can I make breakfast for us tomorrow?"

85.

Of course, I then realized that my former way of giving wasn't really a gift, because it was offered with my considerable expectations. But I only realized these expectations after I experienced the BALANCE in the friendship TIPPING.

I ACTUALLY think I'm more comfortable giving to friends than receiving, because I feel in control when I'm the one giving. I ALSO get the rewards of being perceived as the "good" or "generous" one. I Also means that in any score keeping that may occur, I'll be the "winner." It feels embarrassing to admit this, and also LIBERATING. I know that other people experience this too.

I intend to learn even more about giving that doesn't come from my ego. I will do this by giving anonymously, with an open heart, and without thinking of "fairness" I'M ALREADY practicing this in all of the areas of my life.

it will take lots of practice

86.

receiving in Friendships is **less commonly** Discussed, yet every Giver needs A receiver. For the same reasons Giving can Feel comFortable, receiving can Feel exquisitely unComFortable and unFamiliar.

When I'm receiving in A Friendship, I often Feel vulnerable, needy and out of control. I often silently keep track of How Much, or WHAT I receive, and Measure it AGAinst How Much Feels Safe to Accept.

Most oFten, I'm Already plaaning WHAT to Give BACK As I'm receiving!

This is Also just A Socially AcceptAble WAY of keeping track. It Also indicates An Awareness of WHo Gives and WHo receives.

Some times I'm just GLAD and GrAte. Full to receive!

It is Also A FACT THAT THre Are Givers and THre Are TAkers and We Don't Want To Be THOUGHT of As TAkers.

TAkers and **receivers** Are not THe Same Thing. TAkers Generally Don't pArticipAte in A reciprocal circle.

i THink THAT receivers Are Always enGAGeD As Givers too

To Keep The Circle Going

Giving and **receiving** include qualities like **openness, gratitude, grace** and **Allowing.** It's all energy swirling in a reciprocal circle.

if the giver has no true receiver, there can be no reciprocal circle

We can <u>Become AWARE</u> of whether we're more experienced as givers or receivers, and act accordingly

We can <u>practice</u> receiving without planning what we're going to give back

We can <u>Move easily</u> between receiving and giving without keeping score

We can <u>Transform</u> any score keeping into **B A l a n c e   T e n D i n G**

This focus on receiving and giving will provide a particular kind of **n o u r i s h m e n T** for our friendships. **THIS nourishment will FEED** the vulnerable <u>and</u> strong aspects of ourselves.

SHARING Fresh perspectives

One of THE BEST THings we can DO For and WiTH eACH OTHer As Friends is TO sHAre our perspective WiTH eACH OTHer. We HAVe A view of our Friends THAT THey DON'T HAVe. We DON'T "see" ourselves From THE SAme perspective THAT Friends DO.

i Also Like to cAll it "offering A new view"

Sometimes it HppeNs As A positive CHAllenGe to A Friend. My Friend **McNAir** WAS exCited ABout leAsing A loft spАce to Live aud work in. He HAD DreAmed of THis kind of LOFT SpАce for yers, aud I Felt So exCited to HeAr HiM TАLK ABout THe wood Floors, Floor-to-ceiling windows, aud even A "tower room" in THis one particular loft spАce. We're close Friends, aud sHАre struggles aud suCCesses, so I Asked wHen He would Be Applying For THe spАce, since I knew Applications were Being ACCepted on MONDAY, aud HAD witnessed HiM sometimes DeLAYing DoinG THings He reAlly wanted

He responded to my question by saying:
"I **MIGHT** apply on Monday, but more likely
Tuesday, or at the latest on Wednesday — I
have a lot to do this week."
I took a deep breath and said:

"**MAY** I offer a new view? I don't
understand why you're waiting to apply
for something you want so much. What exactly
is preventing you from applying on Monday Morning?
Are you delaying because you're trying
to do everything perfectly?"

   He sheepishly admitted that he wanted
to wait until he could have a T-shirt made
out of his application that he could then present
to the developer as part of his application package.
McNair is absolutely bulging with creative ideas

I offered that he could still do that
after applying for the loft, and that I thought
his delay was some kind of perfectionistic
sabotage, and that as his **GOOD FRIEND**
I needed to share my perspective.

   He does the same for me!

90.

It FELT A little FRIGHTENING to SHARE MY view WITH HIM, JUST in CASE He WOULD experience it AS interfering with or controlling his process. **PLUS,** WAS it reAlly MY Business?

I THINK THAT WITH Close Friends, we CAN MAKE AGreements About perspective SHARING WITH eACH oTHer and AGree to "MAKE it our Business" WHen we HAVE A VALUABle perspective to offer. In This CASE, I COULDNT Keep silent in THe FACE of THis incredible DREAM prospect, and JUST **Blurted it out.**

After All, He COULD JUST DISAGree, Disregard My view!

McNAir went over on MondAy Morning, MeT THe Developer and is now ensconced in His **DREAM LOFT.**

you can meet him online for teA AT teAwithMcNAir.typepAD.com/

As I walked Around in it For the First Time, I FeLT SVCH **pure Joy** For HiM and GlAD THAT I risKed SHAring My view.

" **If your TrusTeD** people will Allow you to SHAre THeir inner GARDEN, WHAT BeTTer GiFT?" Fred ROGers

91.

THis experience HAS HELPed me to Be BrAver and sHAre My perspectives with oTHer willing Friends.

I FeeL so GRATefuLL For My Friends, WHo sHAre THeir perspectives with me, even if it's not easy or popular. **For example,** My Friend LArry recently Asked me About My Adventures with DAtiNG, which HAve Been MiNiMAL lAtely. I toLD HiM THAT I WAS tAkiNG A BreAk From viewiNG DAtiNG AS BeiNG Like A Job or A Project. He LAuGHiNGly sAid,

"I just reAlly THinK you need someone to **"ring your Bell."**

AnD I sAt up Quickly, Like A DoG sniffiNG THe wiND.

It WAS THe First perspective

i'm GLAD To SAy My Bell is riNGiNG!

THAT HAD intriGued me in A wHile, and I'm Following it to see **wHere it leADs.**

in A non-pressured wAy, of course

92.

Sometimes I feel so automatically resistant to new ideas that it can be challenging for friends to offer a new view.

I remind my friends not to pay so much attention to my resistance— it sounds a lot stronger than it is.

it's actually more like a flimsy fence you can step over or through

I think that most of us initially resist change, and can remind each other to listen beyond any resistance. Our perspectives have great value and can be shared with friends who are interested in growth and change. This is a wonder-full way to nurture our friendships and make them even stronger.

Friendship Nourishment Resources

THE MYTH of You and Me
LEAH STEWART

everyDay matters
Danny Gregory

I KNOW JUST WHAT You Mean
PATRICIA O'Brien
Ellen Goodman

Storypeople.com
eccentric, colorful and Bright place to play

A BIG New Free HAPPY UNUSUAL Life
nina wise

EAT PRAY LOVE
eLIZABETH GILBERT

superherodesigns.com
nourish your soul Here

DannyGregory.com
Creative People At play Here

FUll
BlOOM
Friend
SHip

© SARK '07

JOY
in Friendships

Are your friendships SPARKLING, creative and Vivid?
But not all the time, How annoying!
WHEN They're not, WHAT DO you DO?
WHAT (FRESH) Activities are you doing with friends?

We Forget Fresh
Our friendships L E A P for joy when we attend to them with FRESH new eyes. There is an ALCHEMY between Friends, that I often Forget about.

I wonder, "WHY GET TOGETHER?" "Why not just call or email?"

Then I GET TOGETHER with friends and GASP at what most often occurs. It's the **mixture** of us and them. It **creates** a new entity. We are then enhanced and expanded through experiencing that

97.

entity toGether.

JOY GeTs MUltiplied and MAGnified when you share it.

OUr Friendships Are GreAt vehicles for Joy, and when Joy is witnessed, it Lives on long After The experience HAS conclwded.

> We remember THe JOY
> in Our cells

AnD GO BACK For More.

All of My Friendships Are reliaBle JOY-MUltipliers.

We connect, and JOY HAppens.

I Also experience and observe A lot of Joy in Friendships with online Communities. I created A MESSAGE BOArd in 1998 For people to connect and Form FABulous friendships. It's cAlled the "MArvelous Message BoArd" (MMB) and I invited some of The members to SHAre Their online Friendship experiences in This BOok.

As you reAd Their words, please KNow THAT you Are Also welcome and incwded in Our community.

98.

When I first discovered the MMB, I was in awe of the connections from all around the world. I loved reading about how others had formed friendships, sharing phone calls, snail mail and how they had met in person. I was rather **overwhelmed** at first as the board has so many members and at times I felt very tiny, and easily forgotten. Then slowly I realized that through the written word, I was making connections…and making friends. I found this oddly compelling at first, needing to adjust to a different medium, without facial expressions, without body language…just words to convey how people felt about each other. I found that I was becoming more and more real with all this. My words were always genuine and heartfelt and I received only that in return. I found that I was able to share straight from the heart and able to "listen" effectively to others words, and discovered that doing this forms a basis of very real heart-connections with others. I have shared in the lives and in the very souls of those that I have bonded with here. We learn each other's sense of humour, **our little quirks,** our sore spots, **our heart's yearnings** in a way that often in **real life** gets forgotten.

One thing that I have found to stand out for me in this medium is the sharing of art, writing, crafts…talent in so many forms. In the "real world" I see people afraid to shine, shy about sharing their creativity and their **wondrous unique talents.** And I see people afraid to receive this, too afraid to be inspired by others. I have found that one of the foundations of real friendship is the ability to shine in the presence of others and the ability to bask in the light of others, and shine ourselves, without comparing.

Within an hour, I had "joined" the Society of SARK, but soon after was realizing that most members **seemed** to be young women. My first post was a question: "Men are members here?" I was ready to step back as quickly as I had entered.

A startling thing occurred. I was told that there were men – at least four or five of them active. And then came posts welcoming me. Some were responding to my "bio" and a particular line that intrigued a few people: "I am an ordained minister who **doesn't go** to church."

"In the sweetness of friendship let there be laughter, for in the dew of little things the heart finds its morning and is refreshed" Kahlil Gibran

99.

Those are things that begin to form friendships and then seal them. **Openness.** Honesty. **Trust.** Interest. **Commonality.** Reciprocation. **Listening without Judging. Laughter.** Tears. Forgiveness.

On this huge planet Earth, there is another planet – SARK. Living on the smaller planet makes living on the larger one much more manageable. Each day I can count on being in touch with my friends in Australia, Alberta, Canada, Atlanta, Albuquerque...and those are just the "A" places.

I can support people dealing with cancer, the loss of a parent, a sudden loss of a job or a re-emergence of symptoms of depression or bipolar illness. I can receive support for my writing or my diet and exercise programs. I can be enriched by reading the pages and pages of excellent writing that is simply there **every day.**

"**Succulent Sveva**" speaks about the challenges of having a disease and the advantages and joys of online friendships:

I suffer from a "syndrome" (read disease) that causes my body to be **wracked** with **pain** quite frequently, and very randomly. One day I will be fine (as fine as can be expected) and then the next I can be down so badly that I am in bed all day **crying** because even the blankets hurt me. It also causes me to experience cognitive impairment from time to time, worsening as the pain worsens. **I say all that to say this...**

Face-to-face conversations cause me terrible anxiety at times because sometimes I have difficulty understanding and being understood. Making plans to go out and do things is difficult as I never know from one day to the next how I am going to feel. For this reason, I have found myself holed up in my house avoiding the world.

The MMB has opened up an avenue for me to **make friends** with some lovely people who **genuinely** care about me and how I am feeling, what I am doing. And, of course, this friendship is reciprocated by myself to them. A lot of people have the misconception that you cannot be friends with someone you cannot see or reach out and touch. I beg to differ... What about pen pals? My sister-in-law has had the same pen pal for almost 20 years. They have never "met," but that does not mean they love each other any less. I believe that friends made over the internet, and in particular the MMB, are as real, at least, as the friendships made with pen pals of old.

This is my story of why friendships I have made on the MMB are so important to me. Even on days when I do not feel well enough to get dressed, let alone go out, I can still keep in touch and spread love to them.

100.

"Miraletz" writes about the freedoms in friendship she experiences:

I have forged some amazing **support** networks. Support that many times I do not feel like I get from the people who have been in my life for a long time. I can talk to my MMB friends more candidly sometimes without the **fear** of being judged.

I have discovered new penfriends...in far-off places...magical snails traveling to and fro from Cincinnati to **all corners** of the globe. I have always been a writer and have had pen pals, but usually have formed some sort of other bond prior to exchanging snails...even if it is only the mere fact that we are indelibly connected through SARK...it gives the experience a new twist.

"Deb" speaks about the core group of friends she's made:

The wonderful women I met that night are almost all still part of my life. There is a whole little core group of supportive darlings who have remained connected because of that first spark of the MMB – not just that group from the first PA gathering, but women across the country and indeed across the world.

Our friendships may not be part of our "real" lives, but the connections are real, and priceless, and treasured. The heart doesn't care about geography or distance; I have come to learn that very well. The heart recognizes friendship no matter how far or how different our lives are from each other, and because of these unique and wonderful women, and their friends, my life is immeasurably richer and more vibrant and somehow more secure.

"Phoenix Light" travels to meet MMB friends in person:

This year in March, I am embarking on an adventure to Australia to meet 15 or so of my dear friends from the MMB. I am so excited to meet these people face to face, to give and receive hugs, to **dance** with them in the moonlight, sing, laugh and share stories. Some of these people I do not know deeply, and I look forward to getting to know them better. Some of them I feel I've grown up with...and in a way I have. Some of them I call my sisters and I cannot wait to hold their faces in my hands, and **I know I will cry.** The **meaning** of friendships has become clearer and clearer to me through this new way of "being a friend."

I have learned that it matters little what you wear, how your hair looks, how much you weigh, if you are tall, short or in between. It matters little where you live, what you do for a job, who you are married to or not, or what colour your skin may be, or how much money you have. It matters more what you **share, how you** share, what your heart says, how you listen and respond to others, the kindness you show, the gratitude you feel for the presence of good friends and teachers. And above all else, **love matters most of all.**

OnLine Friendships Are

J OY MULtipliers.
WHeTHer you PArticipAte in My
Online community, or another online
resource, it is exquisiteLY possible
to create and maintain Friendships
WiTHout leaving your Home.

Compound energy Between friends

My Friend Donna and I talk about the amazing nature of this. just like compound _interest_, energy between friends is multiplied over time and through use.

When we have good experiences and share them with friends, I call it compound _energy_, because our experience actually creates good energy for our friend, and then for others.

I might say, "I'm walking three miles a day and eating lots of broccoli." And later my friend says that she felt very inspired to resume swimming and get some organic produce after we spoke. **This energy** between friends travels far, as we each share what we're experiencing and learning, and then it gets magnified and multiplied as it's shared with other friends.

This compound energy is not only for good and joy-full experiences. It works well to expand compassion for times of grief, pain or loss.

I'm continually inspired By How well This works with Friends. A Friend will share WHAT THey're STrUGGLing with, or HAve learned, and THere will Always Be A connecting point Between US wHere we Use compound energy to expand and Grow.

Over and over, I see THAT I AM Awakened, stretched, cHallenged and supported By My Friends energy and THey By Me.

This miracle of compound energy is free and AVAilABle For Friends to Use and Practice. Our Friendships will Flourish with its Use.

Toss THe BAll of energy BACK + ForTH

WHAT can we DO TOGETHER THAT'S
FRESH and exciting? (In Addition to
Movies, dinners, walks, talks...)
Here are some DOTS of POSSIBILITY to
inspire you... CHOOSE A DOT and read THE DE scription on
THE Following pages THAT corresponds

1. ART PLAY

2. Get lOST

3. MAKE MUSIC

4. KINDness Mission

5. Follow A CHILD

6. eAT Meditatively

7. sit in silence

8. Fix or Build SOMETHING TOGETHER

9. Switch CLOTHES

10. Dance to new MUSIC

11. CREATE A PLAY DAY For eAch OTHer
Go To:

12. reAD poetry out loud
MAYA ANGELOU
RUMI
MARY oliver

105.

1. ART Play •

* GATHER some ART MATERIALS: crayons, fingerpaints, pastels or paint. Find any kind of paper. Sit with your friend and just put color on paper. Now TRADE pages and ADD color to each other's creation.
* DRAW A SHAPE, ask your friend to ADD to the shape, and keep trading until it becomes something you can name.
* DRAW or PAINT your friend's FACE, foot or clothing.

2. Get lost •

* Meet your friend somewhere.
* Agree to get lost together.
* WALK or drive somewhere neither you have ever been.
* explore what you find there.

3. MAKE MUSIC •

* GATHER some instruments: DRUM, HARMONICA, guitar, rattle, pots and pans — anything that makes sound.
* YOU and a friend MAKE any kind of music together, especially if it's BAD
* SING a duet or round. Any song will DO.

Go to sabrinawardharrison.com for Abundant inspiration

4. Kindness Mission

TALK with your friend about something kind you can do for others.

Pick a topic.

Set a date.

Do the kind thing.

Discuss how it feels.

5. Follow a Child you already know

You and a friend get together with a child of any age that one of you knows.

* **Follow** that child, go where he or she goes, do what the child does.

Do this for 5 minutes—1 hour and discuss what you observed or learned.

* note: if you are a parent of this child, suspend your parental role as much as possible for this time with your friend

6. Eat Meditatively

Meet a friend for a meal. Eat in silence, noticing all the sounds and tastes.

Do this for 5 minutes—1 hour or longer. Later, talk about how it felt.

7. Sit in Silence

- **ASK** a friend to join you in a silent sit. You might do this somewhere in nature, or inside.
- **Sit** silently for 5 minutes to one hour.
- **Look** at your friend for some part of the time.
- **Let** the silence fill any spaces.
- **Talk** later about how it felt.

8. Fix or Build Something Together

- **Discuss** something each of you needs to fix.*
- **Meet up** and fix each other's one thing.

* Agree to fix things that will take 1 hour or less

9. Switch Clothes

- **When** you get together, agree to switch clothes.
- **Do** this especially if you're different sizes. Adjust the clothes to fit differently. A shirt could become a turban.
- **Talk** about your friendship and clothing and how it felt to switch and experiment.

10. Dance to new music

Play or turn music on, especially unfamilir music.
Dance differently than you ever have.
Fall laughing to the floor.
Talk about how or why dancing is or isnt a part of your life.

11. Create a play day for each other

Send your friend on an adventure, and ask her to do the same for you.
Write an adventure itinerary. (see example next page)
exchange itineraries, by mail or email.
Tell each other the results of your play days.

GO TO LeonieLife.com for soul adventure

12. read poetry out loud

any kind of poetry.
Sit with your friend, in person or by phone.
Take turns reading poetry.
Let the words sit.
Do not speak about the poems unless moved to.

SOUL words + ART

"I give you my word"
A journey to the self through words and watercolor
By Janice Crow

Visit her at STARWAE.com

Send your friend or yourself on An ADventure!

I've created "ADventure itineraries" to support DOing This. **On The next two pages,** you'll FinD A Full DAy and HALf DAy vAriety. **Fill one out** and MAiL it to your Friend, or create your own.

Your Friend **will Be DeLiGHTed and suprised,** and you'll GeT to HeAr About The ADventures THAT occurred. THis is A GooD exAmple of **"Compound energy"** AT plAy, and you and your Friend will BoTH BeneFit By the GooD energy creAted. and All The people THAT Are involved AlonG THe WAy on The ADventure!

ADVENTURE itinerary
SENDING MY FRIEND ON AN ADVENTURE
FULL-DAY VARIETY

WHEN YOU WAKE UP:
- PACK A SMALL BAG WITH: JOURNAL or SKETCHBOOK, WATER, PIECE OF FRUIT OR OTHER SNACK BRING A SWEATER OR JACKET
- WEAR SOMETHING YOU DON'T USUALLY WEAR.
- GO TO _____ AND ORDER THE _____ .
- WALK TO _____ . TAKE OUT YOUR JOURNAL OR SKETCHBOOK AND _____ , _____ .

LUNCH:
- YOU'RE GOING TO _____ ; ORDER _____ OR _____ .

AFTERNOON:
- IT'S NATURE TIME. FIND A TREE AND WRITE A POEM ABOUT IT, OR A DESCRIPTION, OR FIND SOMETHING ELSE IN NATURE TO WRITE ABOUT.

MATINÉE:
- MASSAGE AT _____ , WITH _____ . OR A MOVIE AT _____ .

AFTERNOON TEA OR SNACK FESTIVAL:
- GO TO _____ , AND ORDER _____ .

PLEASURE WALK:
- START WHEREVER YOU ARE AND WALK FOR _____ , THEN LIE DOWN AND SMILE.

CALL OR WRITE ME ABOUT YOUR ADVENTURE!

111.

Adventure itinerary
Sending My Friend on an Adventure
Half-Day Variety

Afternoon
or evening:

Bring a camera or drawing pad
+ notebook, wear a scarf.
You have a reservation at
_____, at _____.

A surprise guest will join you.
He/she will be wearing _____.
You will discuss _____,
and _____.

Take a picture or do a sketch
of this person.

Go to the _____ Museum
at _____. Find a
piece of art that you love.
Write about why you love it, how
it makes you feel.

Go home in a _____, or
_____.

Call or write me about your adventure!

SPENDING MORE SOUL-FULL TIME WITH FRIENDS

SOUL-FULL time DIVES THROUGH THE SURFACE of our Friendships, and touches our souls. "SOUL-FULL TIME" consists of Surprise, DEPTH and spontaneity, and there MAY Also Be some risk.

AS certain kinds of Friendships Grow and Deepen, we MAY Be DRAWN to spend and explore SOUL-Full time together, in ADDITION to our USUAL Friendship Activities.

WE All know How to SHARE A MEAL, Go to A Movie, Go on A WALK or TALK on THE telephone together, and certainly SOUL-Full time can and DOES occur DURING THEse Activities too. WHAT Arsout consciously choosing to spend SOUL-Full time with A Friend or Friends, and Discussing it?

Ask your Friend if THey would enjoy spending THis kind of time Together

113.

There Are Areas in even close friendships THAT sometimes Don't Get Deeply explored in A SOUL·full WAY. THese Are commonly:

- **SEXUALITY**
- **Spirituality**
- **Creative DREAMS**
- **Conflict, Fear**
- **Successes**

One EASY WAY to spend SOUL·full time with Friends is To play A GAME together.

There Are 3 I especially recommend:

1. The transformation GAME
2. The creative DREAM GAME
3. COWGirLS GAME

Details Found in resource section AT end of THis cHApTer

THese GAMes will Bring out Aspects of THe SOUL not previously seen, And encourAGe A Deeper DIALOGue.

read THe "red Book" By SerA BeAK
GreAT WORDS

GAMeS encourAGe SOUL WOrK

I play THESE GAMES FAIRLY often with Friends, and ALWAYS APPreciATE THE SOUL EXPANSION THAT OCCURS. I've DISCOVERED entire planeTS inside Friends THAT I WASN'T AWARE OF, and HAVE experienced MY OWN SOUL in Brand-new ways.

ANOTHER WAY to spend SOUL-full TIME is to PRACTICE "Spontaneous invention" with A Friend. THis is WHere you GET TOGETHer and resolve to DO none of your USUAL ACTiviTIES. THen you invent something new TOGETHer.

MY BROTHER andrew and I CelebRATED THE winter SOLstice in A SOUL-full WAY. THere is A redwood forest near My Home cAlled **Muir woods,** and on THE SOLstice, THE NATIONAL PARK Service LiGHTS candles and BONFires and celebRATes in THE Forest.

115.

ON THIS SOLSTICE NIGHT, IT WAS STORMING and RAINING, and WE DECIDED TO GO anyway.

THERE in THE FOREST, ALL THE PATHS WERE LIT BY luminaria — tiny candles inside of white paper BAGS — and THERE were Thousands of THem. THE GIANT TREES CAUGHT MOST of THE RAIN, and WE WALKED in THE DARK Misty woods By candleGLOW.

THOUSANDS of candles lit

Then **Andrew** SUGGESTED WE Hike up A TRAIL He Knew, and look DOWN to see THE LUMINARIA From ABove.

So we scrambled ALONG THE Muddy TRAIL, Criss-crossed By tree roots,

116.

All BY THE LIGHT of A tiny purple FLASHLIGHT we HAD to SHARE. THis led to slipping, lAUGHing, ADMitting Fear (me) aud feeling soul-fully connected.

And so we cau tumBle suddenly into soul-full times, with Little plauning or discussion. By recognizing when it's HAppening aud stAying There long enoUGH to enJoy THe BenefiTs, we cau Become More AWANe of WHAT soul-full time is, aud leavn to create it aud sHAve it with our friends.

DeAr Friends tumBled suddenly into A soul-full time

JOY LOCATOR WHEEL

TO PLAY BY yourself, or with Friends. Close your eyes, put your Finger Down randomly on A word or phrase, Follow WHAT it says. include This practice in your DAY or night. Notice if There Are repeats of words.

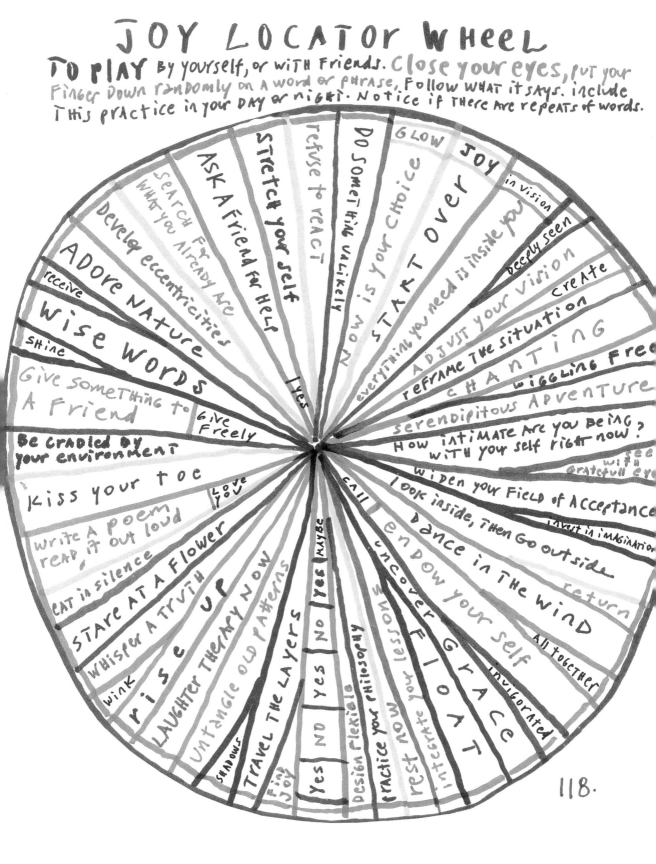

GLOW
JOY
in vision
deeply seen
DO SOMETHING UNLIKELY
refuse to react
Stretch yourself
ASK A Friend FOR HELP
SEARCH FOR WHAT you ALREADY ARE
Develop eccentricities
receive
ADORE NATURE
SHINE
Wise Words
Give SOMETHING TO A Friend
Give Freely
Be cradled by your environment
Kiss your toe
Love you
Write A poem read it out loud
EAT in silence
STARE AT A Flower
Whisper A truth
wink
rise UP
LAUGHTER THERAPY NOW
Untangle OLD PATTERNS
SHADOWS
TRAVEL THE LAYERS
Find JOY
MAYBE
YES
NO
YES
ON
YES
ON
Design Flexibele
PRActice your philosophy
integrate your lesson
rest now less
invigorated
uncover yourself
FLOAT
GRACE
ENDOW your will
DANCE in THE WIND
All together
return
invest in imagination
look inside, THEN Go outside
WIDEN your FIELD of ACCEPTANCE
with GRATEFULL eye
How intimate are you being with your self right now?
serendipitous ADVENTURE
WIGGLING Free
CHANTING
CREATE
ADJUST your Vision
reframe THE situation
Now is your choice
START over
everything you need is inside you
yes
call

118.

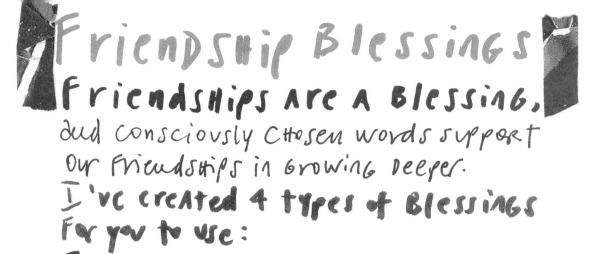

Friendship Blessings

Friendships are a blessing,

and consciously chosen words support our friendships in growing deeper.

I've created 4 types of blessings for you to use:

In Truth and Trust

You use this blessing when you've been friends awhile and wish to solidify a deeper trust.

- **Birth-Day Blessings**

  to celebrate the birth of a friend and to honor their living.

- **Blessings For Sad Times**

  When grief arrives, this blessing acknowledges the sadness and confirms that you stand with them.

- **Ending Friendships with Bravery**

  These words end what was, so that the new can be born. There are 2 versions: one for when you're in a forgiveness process, one for when you're not.

Please freely utilize my words in your friendships, add to them, or create your own. As we write and share these words we feel for our friends, new pathways will open in our hearts and souls.

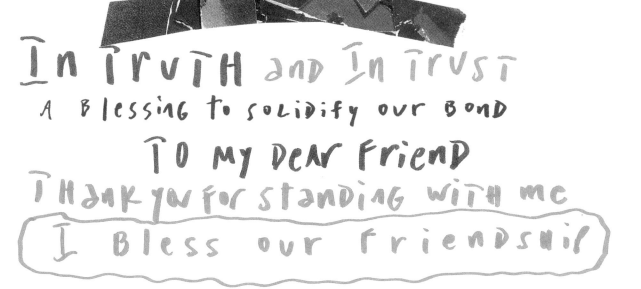

In TRuTH and In TRust

A Blessing to solidify our Bond

TO my DEAr FrienD

THank you for standing WiTH me

I Bless our FrienDsHip

CASE I Feel GrowTH occurs in
THe ease WiTH WHicH we relate.

Discomfort WHen we DisAGree or HAve
conFLicT, I TrusT THAT we
will BuilD new places to stand
toGeTHer. THis is sometimes
uncomfortAble, and I trust
Our process.

Attendance I Feel us compAssionAtely
witnessing eacH oTHer,
THrouGH our cHanGes.
WHeTHer we contact eacH oTHer
or not, I Feel your presence
and Attendance.

JOY We seek places and times to plAy
toGeTHer, and I so vAlue our JOY.

extending

Giving and receiving are not always equal or "fair." I see us both extending ourselves to the other at needed times.

TRUTH

We are committed to TRUTH, even when there is discomfort there. I see us as gently as possible share truths with each other.

TRUST

We have built trust through time and layers of experience. I trust the essence of you. I trust our friendship.

anger

We own our own anger and expressions of it. We do not let anger threaten the basis of our friendship. anger is allowed and respected in our friendship.

commitment

We are committed to TRUTH and growth, and to living in the present moment in our friendship.

124.

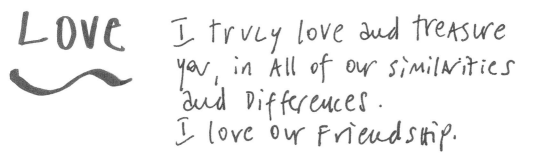

LOVE I truly love and treasure you, in all of our similarities and differences.
I love our friendship.

MAY our friendship continue to evolve and grow, deepen and become even sweeter.
MAY your friendship with yourself expand, and may our paths intersect wherever and however it best lifts and fills us.

i love you

125.

BiRTH DAY BlessiNG

To Honor A Friend's BiRTH and Life

TO MY DEAR FrienD

THank you For BeiNG BorN!

- I AM So DeLiGHTed you Appeared Here, to **froLic** and reveL in Life, AT THe SAMe time As me.
- **MAY your yeAr** Be lovingly Filled WiTH expansive THinKiNG, Deep loving, intuitive ADventuriNG and **unFoLDiNG** of every Description.
- MAY you Fully Know and Feel THe pure value of your Being without performance, proof or resistance.
- MAy you receive Fully and completely, eACH DAy and niGHT, All THAT Fills you.
- **MAY you GiVe** spontaneously without Measure.

126.

MAY you stand (or lie down) in the center of your life, without explanation or apology for who you are in your essence, for the lessons that come as GIFTS, and for your acceptance of those lessons.

MAY you go inside yourself FIRST for Love, and then receive and accept love from others.

MAY candles leap HIGH and WILD at the sight of your SWEET FACE.

Happiest Birthday blessings to you, my endearing friend

127.

Blessings for SAD Times

for offering support in Times of Grief

TO MY Dear Friend

Let me lean in close to you just now.

Let me Honor your SADness and Full HEART.

Let me see your pAin, BecAuse witnessed, it is Lifted.

Let me love you THROUGH THe pAin.

AND, if terror comes, we will roll it BACK TOGETHer to reveal THe wonders VnderneATH.

I Trust your sAdness, and wHye it's TAking and leADing you.

I wish For you...

TO Fully enter and occupy your sADness

TO physicAlly express your pAin

TO receive comFart

TO know truLy THAT you Are not Alone

MAY you Be...

Flexible: and able to allow the comings and leavings of sadness

True: To yourself and your own experience.

Guided: Able to accept direction and support from wise sources

Supported: In truth, release and utter peace

I **HONOR** your sadness and **ACKNOWLEDGE** your journey.

I **stand with you** in these times too.

Your tears Honor the earth.

Allow your falling tears, the unexpected rise of laughter and the deep-knowing that you are **utterly safe** in your sadness.

129.

eNDING FriENDSHips WiTH BrAVeRY

Friendships end fr All sorts of reAsons. Sometimes it feels like A nAturAL enDinG, sometimes it Hurts too MVCH to continue to Try and Be friends, and THere is Benefit in Assisting it to end. **FriendsHips** Are not often given THe KinD of Assistance wiTH concwding THAT oTHer types of relationships receive. WiTH Friendships, we Are encourAGeD to Just "let it Go" or ForGeT WHAT HurT. **Most of us** Just stop communicAtinG WiTH THAT PARticulAr Friend, and THen MAy DrAG any unresolved pAin into our next Friendship.

I THink THAT THe BrAvery in endinG Friendships is connected to THe AllowinG and Acceptance of friendships ending and CHANGinG. **I've Felt** WHAt Appens to Be THe opposite of BrAve wiTH reGArd to Friendships endinG. I've Felt Frustrated, Discouraged, **Furious,** confused, puzzled, lost and upset.

Luckily usually not all at once!

Mostly, I've had considerable difficulty letting go. I'm a pretty sentimental, loyal and sometimes obsessive sort of person and have assumed that friends were the same. I've learned that friendships are both sturdy and fragile, and can end for reasons that have very little to do with me!

"If you want a happy ending, that depends of course, on where you stop your story"

Orson Welles

What about when you want to end the friendship?

I've written two types of letters you can use to conclude friendships. One is to use when you are feeling love and forgiveness towards your friend, the other for when you are not.

These letters do not need to be sent to be effective energetically

I've experienced powerful shifts with former friends by doing this kind of letter writing. **You can also** speak your ending out loud with or without a friend, and it will have great effect.

You might choose to use parts of what I've written, or some words may inspire you to write your own letter. Perhaps you'll write words in your journal, or on paper that you will burn.

Maybe you will just read the letters inside this book and something will soften and shift inside your heart.

Our hearts are made for softening and breaking

(To use when you are feeling love & forgiveness towards
your friend and if there has been previously unresolved pain)

Dear _____,

Thank you for your presence in my life.
We shared such richness.

I feel guided to say goodbye to you, to
our former friendship, and to complete the circle
we began as friends.

It is clear now that we are no longer friends,
and I wish to speak about it and honor what we
shared, rather than waiting for time and distance
to fade our connection.

I wish to write consciously and directly
of our friendship ending, celebrate and acknowledge
the friendship we shared, and say Thank you
for all the kindnesses and love you extended
to me. Please feel free to communicate
further if you wish. You can reach me at _____.

I consider our friendship to have been a
true blessing, and this completion honors that
blessing.

I truly wish you the best of everything,
and in everything. I send you peace.

love, _____.

(To use when you are feeling angry, sad, hurt or unforgiving towards your friend)

Sometimes when I feel hurt or angry, I disappear, or avoid what hurts. I'm choosing to communicate about this time in our friendship differently.

I'm letting you know that I'm experiencing pain in our friendship, and I'm going to explore this pain by myself until or if, it's time to communicate with you again, knowing this time may never come.

I'm letting go of our friendship.

This may be final, or there may be more for us to explore together, I'm not sure.

Please know that I'm grateful for the good things in our friendship, and what we shared.

I wish you well.

Friendship Blessings resources

real Life rituals
Karyl Huntley

I Thought We'd never Speak Again
Laura Davis

Forgive for Good
Dr. Fred Luskin

emotional Blackmail
Susan Forward p.H.D. with Donna Frazier

Perfect love, imperfect relationships
John Welwood

LifeChallenges.org
A place to Find support for All sorts of Transitions

Life Makeovers
Cheryl Richardson

Woman's retreat Book
Jennifer Louden

"A true friend is somebody who can
make us do what we can"
    Ralph Waldo Emerson

Chapter seven

Questions
to ask friends
and
Tributes
to
friends

"I awoke with devout Thanksgiving
for my friends"
    Ralph Waldo Emerson

Questions to Ask Friends

Your friends have things to say about you and your friendship that you haven't heard yet. So many good words in friendships are unspoken, and challenging observations often remain unsaid. Yet we are continually growing and changing, and we can benefit from new perspectives in our friendships.

Asking questions about friendship opens up new dialogue between friends. I discovered this when I asked some of my close friends the following questions:

137.

1. **Describe** our friendship and what it means to you.

2. **What** are some of your favorite or funny things about our friendship?

3. **What** do you find challenging or difficult about being friends with me, or about our friendship?

4. **What** have you learned from our friendship?

I felt surprised, gratefull and closer to each of my friends after sharing our answers to these questions, and I learned a lot about myself and about my friends.

You can ask and answer these questions verbally with a friend, and there's also **something magical** about writing down your answers and reading theirs— the written word enters the heart in a different way.

I will caution you to ask and answer number three with sensitivity and kindness as well as **truth.**

your truth

138.

I ADMire You...

I spend Time Acknowledging and ADMiring My friends, and They me. We do This By witnessing each other's lives, and Then offering reflections BACK To each other About WHAT we see and experience. This Attendance To TruTH and GROWTH AWAKENS new DiALOGVE Between us. We don't spend our Time idealizing each other, BuT rATHer seeing each other's successes, FAilures and struggles WiTH loving eyes.

I Also Believe in creating written tributes to friends Because The Words HAVE SuCH A power-full long-lasting effect, and This ADDS More friendship DepTH. I don't Think we Honor and Acknowledge our friendships As MucH or As often As They Deserve. I've seen friends GAin SucH STREnGTH from reading A Tribute To Them.

Here Are Some of My current tributes WITH SPAce For You to ADD tributes to Your own DeAr friends.

139.

TO MY FRIEND YOFE

Being friends with you

is like having my own personal sunshine. Your face is lit by love and your life-loving energy feeds everyone. I admire you for so many reason. For your patience with Human Beings, and your friendships with elders. For teaching yoga to young children, and for all the love you share through your Therapeutic Massage practice. For your endless enthusiasm, for parties, activities and playing in so many dimensions. For swimming in the San Francisco Bay and inviting me to join you even though I always say NO. I appreciate your impatience with rules that don't make sense, your commitments to people who need help, and your involvement with your friend's lives. I see you growing and changing, becoming deeper and more truly your self. I hear you when you share rarely what you don't like about your life. I celebrate your growth and changes and am Honored you are my friend.

140.

TO MY FRIEND JOSHUA

Being Friends With You

is like a red speedBoat on an Alpine Lake. Your Joy-full participation in Life is refreshing and Full of wonder. I ADMIRE YOU for the music that's in your soul that comes through your beauti-full hands and Lips. Your endless Questing for truth and sometimes justice: For your whimsical and stubborn nature, for how well you wear a towel as a turban, For letting Go of whatever doesn't serve your essence. I Appreciate your enthusiastic Messages and Listening To me, your countless kindnesses and Being curious About what Life can teach you. I see you leaving eGo Behind and Living compassionately with yourself and others. I Hear you as you work through old patterns, and then laugh deLightedly. I celebrate All that you've let Go of, and All that you've let in. I feel SO Blessed By our Friendship.

141.

TO MY FRIEND MARNEY

Being friends with you is like finding out who the pinball wizard _is_. Your "creative fountain" life nourishes me and so many others. <u>I admire you</u> for the incredible journey you've taken, the lifting of emotional veils and your willingness to see and be seen. I admire your focus, your inventiveness and your giant heartlight. I admire your marriage and how you support each other. <u>I appreciate</u> your keen memory, quirky humor and allegiance to creativity. I appreciate your deep listening and well of laughter. <u>I see you</u> committed to growth and change, and shifting even more into solid center. <u>I hear you</u> when you speak of what still isn't working. <u>I celebrate</u> your courage and willingness, and feel so grateful for our friendship.

142.

TO MY FRIEND ANDREA

BEING FRIENDS WITH YOU is LIKE HAVING ACCESS TO A 24 HOUR TOY STORE. YOUR EXUBERANCE and ZESTY APPRECIATION FOR LIFE and ART is PURE JOY. **I ADMIRE YOU** for your WRITING, your PHOTOGRAPHS, and BECOMING A LIFE COACH. I ADMIRE YOU FOR YOUR WILLINGNESS TO LIVE JOY-FULLY and TALK OPENLY ABOUT WHAT HURTS. I ADMIRE YOUR MARRIAGE and YOUR CREATIVE DREAMS. **I Appreciate** YOUR MINIATURE PIGTAILS and THAT YOU OFTEN WEAR LIME GREEN. I APPRECIATE YOUR ATTRACTION TO THE UNUSUAL, and THAT WE CAN BOTH ADMIT CERTAIN THINGS ABOUT THE WORLD THAT WE DON'T KNOW. **I see you** STEPPING MORE FULLY INTO YOUR POWER and LIVING CONFIDENTLY AS YOURSELF. **I HEAR YOU** WHEN YOU TALK ABOUT YOUR RAW, REAL PAIN. **I celebrate** HOW FULLY YOU OCCUPY YOUR LIFE, and THAT WHEN YOU READ THIS, YOUR BRAND-NEW BABY WILL BE HERE!!! I AM **SO GLAD** WE ARE FRIENDS.

143.

CORY THIS PAGE or USE iT To MAKe your own tribute fr A Friend

TO MY Friend

Being Friends WiTH you

I ADMire you

I Appreciate

I see you

I Hear you

I celebrate

DO YOU THINK you're A Good Friend? WHY or WHY not?

In MY CONVERSATIONS WITH people ABout This topic, I've Uncovered A few Themes:

MOST people DescriBe Themselves As A Good Friend Most of THE Time.

Some people Dont consider Themselves To Be A Good Friend on A consistent BAsis.

MOST people HAve incrediBly HiGH StandArds for THEir own Friendship ABiLities, and less for THEir friends.

ALMost everyone considers it very important to (Be) and HAve Good Friends.

My friendsips Allow me THE SPAce to explore and experience MAny QuALities and WAYS of Being. Sometimes, I Find MyseLf trying To Be A friend cAlled "ideAL susan" portrAying All of my "positive" QuALities, and none of THE "neGAtive" ones. Of course,

"A friend Loveth At All times." Proverbs 17:17

145.

THis never works Because I'm just HuMAN and MAGnificently Flawed.

I THiNK I'M A pretty Good Friend, Most of THe TiMe, and THis is Finally enough For me. I've leArned THAT I don't need to prove anyThing to My Friends or GAin THeir love and Approval By "performing" or Being some WAY THAT I'm not.

Here is My AssessMent (PARTIAL, of course) **of Myself** As A Friend to OTHers, WiTH A little Help From pAsT and present Friends.

I Believe it's VALuABle to MAKe THese AssessMents As We Grow and Develop Our Friendship CAPACities. **writing Down** or speAKing ABout our positive and CHAllenGing QuALities Allows us to **expand WHAT works well**, and choose Differently For WHAT Doesn't. **Over THe YeArs,** I've Been told By Friends THAT I'M S O M e T i M e s :

146.

Pushy

Ungrateful

Narcissistic

Selfish

Bossy

Difficult

Picky

Moody

Self-Absorbed

resistant

Unforgiving

over sensitive

Formidable

controlling

Prickly

indecisive

uncommitted

Tantrumic
prone to tantrums

Attitudinal

compulsive

Obsessive

Fixated

Judgmental

punitive

annoying

Aggravating

negative

"WHO Are your Friends?" you ASK. "HOW COULD THey Describe you in These WAys?" I ASK Friends To tell THe TRUTH, and I AGree THAT I sometimes exHiBit THese Qualities—especially in close, Deep friendships. I've Also Been TOLD By Friends THAT I'm S O M e T i M e s:

147.

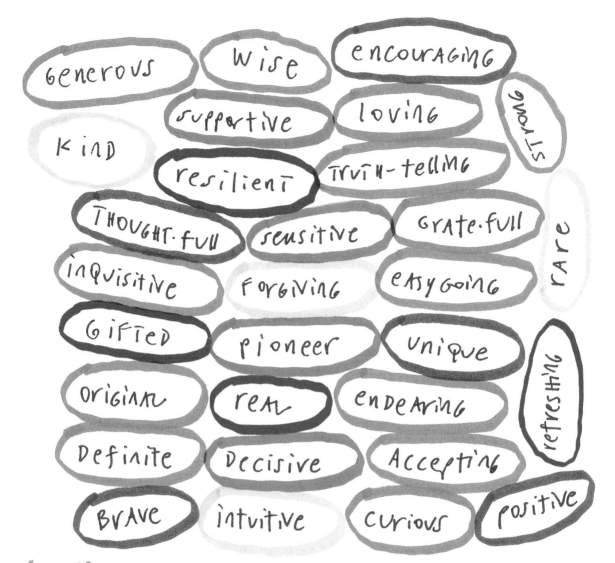

generous   Wise   encouraging

supportive   loving   strong

Kind

resilient   truth-telling

rare

THOUGHT·full   sensitive   Grate·full

inquisitive   forgiving   easygoing

Gifted   pioneer   unique

original   real   endearing   refreshing

Definite   Decisive   Accepting

Brave   intuitive   Curious   positive

You'll notice THAT MOST OF MY "CHALLENGING"
Qualities show up as opposites in the "positive"
Qualities. I THINK THAT THIS is True for MOST
of us. I've learned THROUGH Friendship
THAT I'm not A polarized caricature of one or
The other, But An AMALGAM of BOTH.

148.

Do you think you're a Good Friend?
an Assessment

Fill in the spaces with words you've <u>sometimes</u> been told you are:

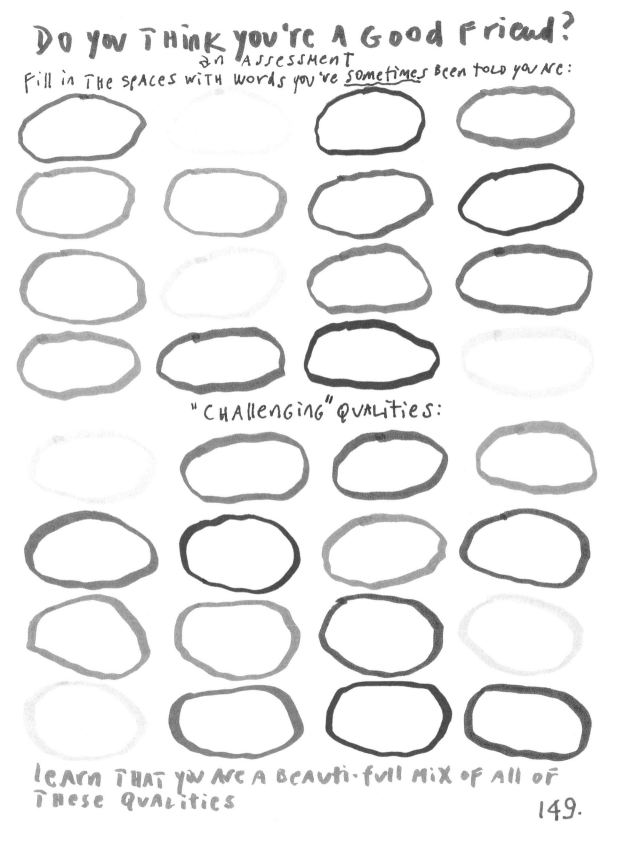

"CHALLENGING" Qualities:

learn that you are a beauti·full mix of all of these qualities

149.

Questions to Ask Friends, and tributes to Friends resources

The rule of Two
Ann Woodin
Drawings By
Andrew Rush

Ask and it is Given
Esther and Jerry Hicks

Love is letting go of Fear
Gerald Jampolsky

power of now
Eckhart Tolle

Loving what is
Byron Katie

Passionate presence
Catherine Ingram

Abraham-Hicks.com
Home of
The Abraham
Teachings

Conscious Living
Gay Hendricks

Succulent Wild Woman/Man
Gatherings

When I wrote a book called "Succulent Wild Woman" in 1997, it was my statement of self-liberation. It's all about a person <u>feeling fully free to express themselves in every dimension of their life</u>

> ## To Be Succulent:
> To Live ripe, Juicy, whole, round, exuberant, wild, rich, wide, deep, firm, rare Lives

People began connecting and forming Succulent Wild Woman (SWW) and Succulent Wild Man (SWM) Groups all over the world. It has become a way to connect, meet and make friends eccentrically and **not typically.** These Gatherings are as varied as the people are. They are not all about wearing glitter, boas, tiaras or pajamas—although some are. It's more about being **succulent** together in whatever form that takes.

Here are some comments from some of the people who've grown from attending SWW or SWM Gatherings:

Kim writes about her SWW group:

5 years ago I answered a post to start a SWW. I was **new** to the area and didn't know a soul so I decided to jump right in. I invited the three women who answered to come to my home for a meeting. We followed the suggestions from the SWW book for getting started and although it was **scary,** we made it through. Over the next few months the group grew to seven wonderful women. Although we've had our challenges, we've started a **journey** that has carried us to some wonderful friendships and a monthly meeting of laughter, tears, **succulence** and soul for the past five years.

"FiFi Bear" writes about her succulent gathering:

We called it a goddess evening. My daughter (aged 11) and I went shopping for goddess food, and inspiring and creative "bits." Then she and a friend decorated our lounge room with candles, glitter and purple (waterproof) tablecloths. As my friends arrived each was greeted with a bubbly cocktail. During the evening each person was presented with a **blank** notebook and invited to decorate the front cover. This was what the creative "bits," all stacked in a gorgeous cane basket, were for. Once our books had time to dry I asked each person to write their name at the top of the first eight pages (we had nine people there). Next we passed the books around the group, each writing something for the named person on the page. In some we offered words of wisdom and gratitude, the names of singers or books we thought the person should listen to or read, or we told stories and shared memories. This was an evening of immense laughter and love and one of the best birthday celebrations I have ever enjoyed!

"PHARMA in THE FALLS" resolved to ADD SUCCULENCE To Her Life:

We shared a lot about our lives, our families, our grief and despair and our individual accomplishments. When I had been on the Board about 6 months or so I agreed to meet some of the people I had been so frequently chatting with. So, I popped myself into my car (resplendent with balloons and a bright pink piece of Bristol board in the back window that said **"The Dharma NOT GOING TO TURN INTO A SMALL TOWN MOM Tour 2000"**)....I was off on a big adventure. I was driving two days to meet a dozen women I had never laid eyes on. The only information I had was the time of our meeting and the name of a Mexican restaurant in some small town in Pennsylvania I had only map directions to.

What a night! Such laughter and smiling eyes and friendship! I have retained some of those **friendships** for over 6 years now. Emails, telephone calls, still posting back and forth to one another...

"ISSA" reflects THAT SUCCULENCE is Also in THE CHANGED PLANS AND MOODS:

It's funny because we had so many plans for the evening and the morning after....things we wanted to do, like make tiaras and dance....but as it turns out, we assumed our places around a large table with lots of yummy snacks and drinks (Shannon made cookies that looked like little hats!) and we quite literally didn't budge all night long until it was time for bed! We just couldn't stop talking. I loved that we ranged in age as women, but still connected with lots to learn from each other....we talked about self-image, romance, friendships....the funny thing is, we all admitted to having had second thoughts about coming to it....thinking "oh, we're so busy, it'll be hard to take time out for just something social, etc."—and we laughed about how we were so glad we ignored that little voice and went anyway!

"SOMETIMES OUR LIGHT GOES OUT BUT IS BLOWN INTO FLAME BY ANOTHER HUMAN BEING. EACH OF US OWES DEEPEST THANKS TO PEOPLE WHO HAVE REKINDLED THIS LIGHT" ALBERT SCHWEITZER

155.

HAVE A PALOOZA!
WHAT it is, HOW TO HAVE One

I've asked some of the members of the Marvelous Message Board to share their "PALOOZA" experiences, to inspire you to have your own.

PALOOZA:
- A fun party, either prenranged or spontaneous

  or

- expanding something fun into something more fun!

"THE DISH" A <u>renowned</u> palooza & party-giver writes about HOW TO THROW A PALOOZA:

How To Throw a Palooza ~
I have hosted what I declare to be two successful slumber parties:
Dishapalooza 2003 and Dishapalooza II 2004 (2za).

Use Evite to invite people, organize the guest count, etc.
Ask everyone to bring their own blankets, pillows, sleeping bags, etc.
Ask everyone to bring a dish (and a Dish).
Tell people to just show up in their pjs.
You supply the plates, napkins, utensils and possibly the drinks (you can always order pizza too).
Set up a "quiet room" or area. I did this and no one really used it. I had candles and hand lotion and blankets and stuffed animals in there for people who needed to get away for a few minutes and breathe.
Have someone do readings (you'll want a quiet semi-private/private spot for this too).
If people drink alcohol, BE ADAMANT ABOUT NO DRINKING & DRIVING!
Have something for breakfast -- keep it simple! Or better yet -- go out to breakfast in your pjs!

Purchase inexpensive party favors:
http://www.planetsark.com/community_groups_succulent_ww_guide.htm
Get a catalog sent to you -- so many neat things/inspirations. I ordered tiaras and magic wands for everyone.

Think **SUCCULENCE** when decorating. I ordered 10 feather boas from eBay ($30) and draped them on the banisters and bookcases. I spun silver stars (the kind on wires) around the railings. Hang lights. Use lots of candles. Use sidewalk chalk and write messages on the front porch. I wrote MAGIC to let everyone know what they were about to step into.

Ask everyone to bring a little gift for everyone (this can be super inexpensive things -- or handmade or painted rocks or colorful leaves, stickers, super balls).

Get a pack of SARK's Juicy Living cards. Let everyone pick one to keep.

Use name tags! Let everyone make their own.

Remind everyone to bring their cameras.

ASK FOR HELP!

Do a gift exchange. Everyone brings a gift for the exchange (maybe $20 max). You can do the "stealing game," though we voted on it this time and the consensus was NO STEALING! We picked names and said something nice about the person. I went first and got MercyUnique. I acknowledged her, she then picked a gift, opened it and then chose the next name. She acknowledged that person and so on and so on.

Leave out crayons, markers, paper, etc.

Have a show and tell.

Play ice breaker games "getting to know you games" especially if it's the first gathering.

Have music. Ask people to bring Cds.

Give up all expectations.

Give up that it has to look or be a certain way. Not everyone expresses joy, happiness and enthusiasm the same way. Trust that everyone is having fun and is responsible for their own fun!

Be sure to thank the host profusely. Let her know that you had a magical time.

I'm sure I'll think of more and I'm SURE others can contribute to this too.

Most importantly, RELAX and HAVE FUN!

"Diva Butterfly" writes about deliciously attending the palooza:

I had the pleasure of attending Dish's Dishapalooza2 (also known as 2za) in October of 2004. I had the best time seeing the **shocked** looks on the faces of others as I told them I was flying to California for a weekend, just for a slumber party with a bunch of people I'd never actually met! LOL

I got to stay with the beautiful Dancing Mermaid in her Goddess guest room, as well as partying with the rest of the Palooza guests in attendance at Dish's. They were all so kind to me as I wasn't feeling very well, and I **crashed** kind of early. There was karaoke, gift exchanging, butt slapping, and going out for breakfast in our PJ's! It was a very special time, and it allowed me to connect even more closely with some of the people on the message board. These women have been key to the maintenance of my mental health since my Mom passed away; they've all invited me to come visit, offering me a place to stay, and just held my hands through the **dark moments.** I thank you every day for the creation of the MMB, as it's something **unique** and **beautiful.**

157.

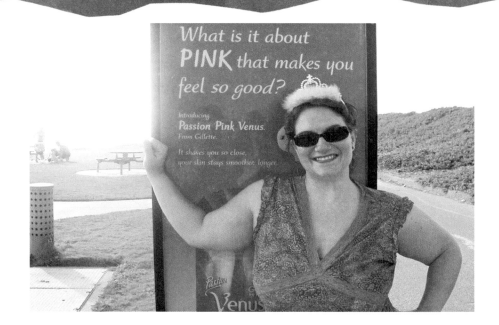

Kim Writes About The Pink Party:

My **favorite** was our Pink Party. The day couldn't have been more perfect. Cynthia had gone out early in the morning to **save us** a bonfire pit on the beach and we'd all committed to doing everything PINK for the next 16 hours. Why pink? We wanted something to take us out of our usual routine and most of us weren't really pink-wearing women. So we dressed in pink; Tiffany had a gorgeous pink vintage dress, Julie bought pink bindhi jewels for our faces and I brought some pink maribou tiaras. We knew the day was meant to be when we saw the advertisement for passion pink venus razors next to our fire pit. It read, "What is it about Pink that makes you feel so good?" We drank cosmopolitans and pink lemonade and made the people who wandered by wonder. We frolicked in the ocean until the sun went down and then Cynthia pulled out her guitar and we sang every song we could remember and danced around the bonfire. We walked back to the car arm in arm and put on our pink pjs for a night of laughter and very little sleep! Overall it was **pinkalicious** and it's made me smile every time I wear something pink ever since!

WHETHER YOU CALL IT A "PALOOZA" OR FOLLOW ANY OF THESE SUGGESTIONS, WHAT MATTERS MOST IS THAT YOU GATHER WITH "KiNDRed spirits" for

- inspiring conversations,
- WiLD LAUGHTer,
- Creative communion,

and JUST HAVING FUN WITH OTHER people.

We Are ALL inspired By THe UNUSUAL, Unexpected, UNCOMMON Times.

Let your Friendship Life Be FULL of THese kinds of experiences.

in progress GATHERINGS
Friends supporting Forward Movement

My Friend Audrea told me about a group she's attended called "in progress" where people GATHER to discuss whatever they're currently working on, or playing with. The group supports each other to continue to **MAKE progress** — tiny or large. I think this is an inspiring way for friends to get together and

create Movement

Here are my suggestions:

ASK a few friends if they'd like to join you for an "in progress" GATHERING. You might call it something else too. Here's a description you might use:

---

in progress

Join us in a SALON ATMOSPHERE (comfortable seating, refreshments)

Bring something (either literally or figuratively) you'd like to make progress with, for a FUN, nonjudgmental, no-pressure supportive GATHERING to move your project forward

Bring a notebook + pen and something to eat or drink that can be shared

note: THE TIME MAY inspire you!

160.

Decide if you'd like to ACT AS FACILITATOR for THE GATHERING. If so, Here Are Some Guidelines:

Invite 3 to 6 people to your Home or OTHer COMFORTABLE SPACE.

Define THE GATHering with A Description of WHAT you'll Be Doing TOGETHer and How you'll Be MAKing progress.

Give each person 10-15 Minutes to tAlk About THeir project or idea — WHATever THey'd Like to MAKE progress WiTH.

ASK each person to spend 5-10 Minutes writing Down WHAT's Blocking THeir progress

THe Group will THen Hear WHAT BLOCKS each person's progress and MAKE "Solution SUGGestions." The person WHose project it is TAKes notes and each person THen TAKes A turn

Conclude THe GATHering By each person
* NAMing THe progress THey experienced MAKing

* very unLikely. But if someone still feels stuck, spend 5-10 Minutes As A Group Discussing WHAT oTHer steps May work

Schedule another "in progress" GATHering for THose WHo Liked it and would Like to GeT TOGeTHer AGAin.

161.

reminders for friends
Attending in progress GATHerings

- **"More" progress isn't "Better"**
  This is not a progress competition. It's a way to support forward movement, and this forward movement can be **any size** to be of value.

- **Don't COMpare**
  Someone else's progress is none of your business, in the sense of comparison. Also, no comparing yourself to others!

- **Be clear and concise**
  When offering FEEDBACK, brevity will work well for purposes of progress.

- **Be receptive**
  When receiving FEEDBACK, TAKe notes and ASK questions in a receptive Manner.

- **resolve unanswered questions**
  Before leaving the GATHering, clear up any confusion or questions about whatever is needed

SHARE and Tell
Friends Sharing Great stuff

Friends tease me sometimes when They visit, Because I often have Things to show and tell, and They say it reminds Them of Kindergarten. I've Attended several Gatherings we've called "**Share and tell**" So that friends can Be Together, sharing what They love and telling about it too.

ASK your friends to come over for "share and tell." You Might use This Description:

Share something good with your friends!
Tell us a story About Where it came From, How you Made it, etc.
Bring your sharing object or _____, to My House on _____ At _____.
you can share anything you'd Like: Something you Made, Something Someone gave you, an Animal, A car, A person, Something to eat, A creative project, A Slide show. A Musical instrument, or WHATever.
each person gets _____ Minutes to Share+tell.
_{Figure out THE TiME By THE number of people Attending.}

Be prepared for an uplifting, tender, humorous, hilarious and educational time.

Remember to invite only as many people as you have time for—each person getting 30 minutes to share adds up quickly.

You could of course, invite more people and give them each 15 minutes

When I attended Leigh's share and tell, I SAT in AWE as people shared photo albums, homemade musical instruments, paper dolls, pieces of art and one tiny turtle.

one tiny turtle

THE STORIES shared that night were fascinating.

My friends surprised me with the depth and detail of what they shared, and I found out so many things I didnt know. Spending time sharing and telling like this reminded us all of the best parts of being a child—and we didnt need to be in school to do it!

164.

ʻARTRAGEOUS ART parties for Friends

THE PURPOSE OF AN ARTRAGEOUS GATHERING, IS TO

PLAY

TOGETHER

AS ADULTS, WE OFTEN ASK, "WHAT'S THE POINT?" In THIS GATHERING, THE <u>point</u> is TO <u>PLAY</u>.

- **S**ET UP A PLAY AREA
- **U**SE CARD TABLES, OR PICNIC TABLES, OR WHATEVER TABLES CAN BE COVERED and USED FOR ART
- **C**OVER THE FLOOR WITH A TARP OR recycled newspapers
- **S**ET UP THE TABLES LIKE A "BUFFET OF ART"

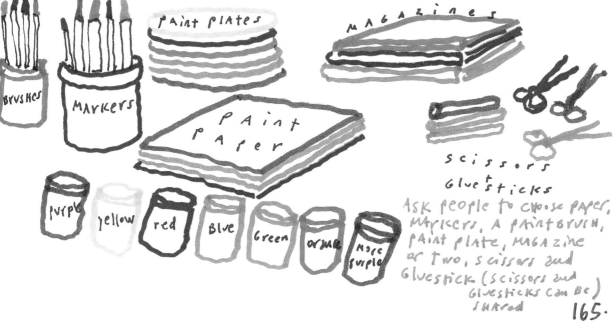

BRUSHES MARKERS PAINT PLATES MAGAZINES

PAINT PAPER

scissors
gluesticks

purple yellow red Blue Green orange More purple

ASK PEOPLE TO CHOOSE PAPER, MARKERS, A PAINT BRUSH, PAINT PLATE, MAGAZINE or TWO, SCISSORS and GLUESTICK (SCISSORS and GLUESTICKS CAN BE) SHARED

165.

A. ll
R. eady
T. o play!

Here are some simple, fun ways to get started making art with your friends:

Here's your supply list

These can be very inexpensive, you can also ask friends to bring some

* **Paper** any kind, sizes like 8 x 10, 9 x 12, 18 x 24
* **Markers + pens** thick, thin, multi-colored
* **Paint** + water containers + brushes + rags + water source + paper plates
* **Old magazines** any kind
* **Scissors + gluesticks** enough for each, or just a few to share

Send an invitation, or just call friends

Let's make some ART together!

Come over for some coloring, Collage, painting and **expressing** yourself

• Only playing, no professional process or product

Wear something that can get paint or gluestick on it

Please bring ———, ———, ———.

GAME #1 Pleasure of painting

* **Paint on paper** using fingerpaints or paint with brushes, put color onto paper
* **Trade paper** switch papers and ADD color to someone else's
* **Tear paper** Tear up WHAT you painted and turn it into SOMETHING else By Gluing The pieces onto another piece of paper

THIS GAME gets color moving and removes the "Finished" idea about ART

GAME #2 Drawing for everybody

* **Drawing each other** Two people Face each other. Each draws the other without looking at the paper, OR lifting up their pen/marker
* **Share portraits** write The Name of The person you Drew and HAVE A "GAllery" show. Set up The pictures and ADMire Them AS A Group
* **ADD Description** on The BACK of The portrait you DREW, write WHAT you ADMire About How The person Actually looks to you

THIS GAME inspires DRAWING WHAT you see and letting The lines play with SHAPES

167.

GAME #3 everyone collages

- **COLLAGE A COVER** USING MAGAZINES, CUT or rip out IMAGES, colors or words THAT APPEAL to you.

- **FOLD PAPER** into A SQUARE, THIS CAN Be your COVER FOR A BOOK. THIS BOOK CAN BE USED FOR ANYTHING you'd LIKE: A JOURNAL, GRATITUDES, COMPLAINTS, PHOTOGRAPHS or RANDOM THOUGHTS.

- **ADD** inside PAGES to your BOOK. SHARE your COLLAGE COVERS with everyone

<u>I</u>f you LIKED MAKING ART with friends and **PLAYING** TOGETHER, you CAN HAVE another GATHERING. **CHOOSE** A SUBJECT or topic and Meet AGAIN. **YOU MIGHT** DRAW or PAINT A MODEL or OBJECT, or TAKE A Trip to A MUSEUM toGETHER. You MIGHT Also pick A NAME for your ART GATHERING

SUCH AS:

"DOING it BADLY and HAPPILY ART Group"

SALONS and Soirees

Are so appealing because of their private nature and history.

I THINK of velvet curtains, mahogany booths, candlelight or miniature lanterns...

Any table or place

Can become a salon or soiree

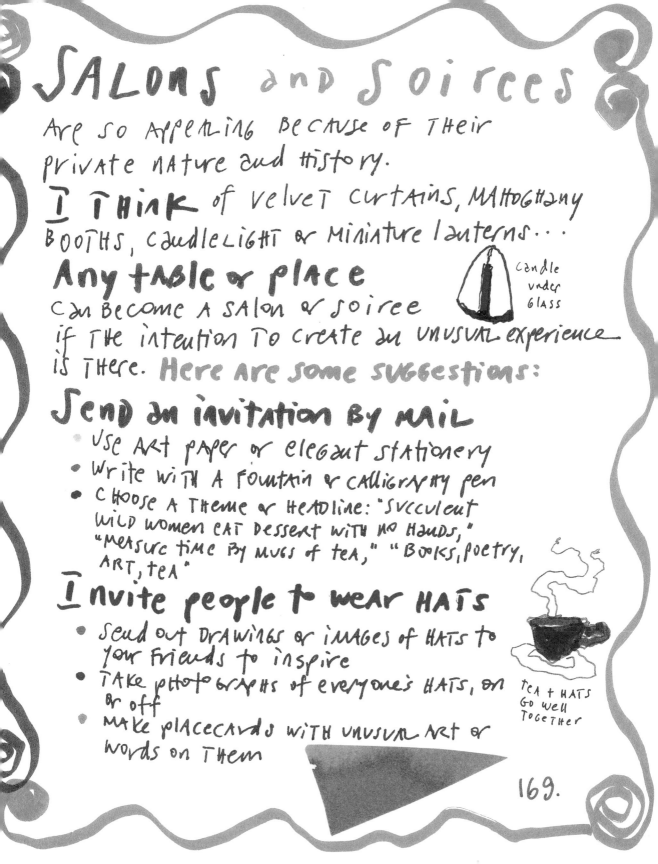

Candle under glass

if the intention to create an unusual experience is there. **Here are some suggestions:**

Send an invitation by mail

- Use art paper or elegant stationery
- Write with a fountain or calligraphy pen
- Choose a theme or headline: "Succulent wild women eat dessert with no hands," "measure time by mugs of tea," "Books, poetry, art, tea"

Invite people to wear hats

- Send out drawings or images of hats to your friends to inspire
- Take photographs of everyone's hats, on or off
- Make placecards with unusual art or words on them

Tea + Hats go well together

169.

HAve Delicious snAcks and teAS

- offer A selection of cAFFeine-Free teAS ded CAFFeinAted and oTHer liquid refreshment THAT isut teA
- HAve DesseRTs, incluDing svcculeut FRvit
- offer A Bit of protein: cHeese, HAVd-Boiled egGs or sHRimp

YOV CAN HOST A SAloN, SoiRee or HiGH teA AT your Home or AT A restAuRant. THe conversAtion will Be inspired By THe ATMosphere and Costumes.
lAte AfternooN is A lovely Time For HiGH teA . . .

Some kinDs of men will Appreciate THis kinD of GATHeriNG dad Like to Be incuDed, oTHer types will Be GlAD Not to Be incwDed.

All Types Like teA

170.

eccentric Friendship GATHering resources

CREATIVITYPORTAL.COM
explore and express your creativity with friends in this vibrant community

ZEROGDANNO.COM
Great ideas for Art parties + Gift + craft ideas

A LITHGOW PALOOZA
101 ways to entertain and inspire your kids (or inner kids)
JOHN LITHGOW

LITHGOW PARTY PALOOZAS
52 unexpected ways to make a Birthday, Holiday or any Day a Celebration
JOHN LITHGOW

KARENDRUCKER.COM
Music "STRAIGHT TO THE SOUL" for friendships everywhere

Creativepostcardclub.com
connect with other "SNAIL MAIL" enthusiasts

JOSHUAKADISON.COM
Music for your Great Big spirit and Gatherings of friends

TheArtistsway.com
ideas and ways to creatively connect with your friends

The ART of
eXTRAVAGant LoUNGinG with FrienDS

LoUNGinG with Friends is
pleasurable, but extravagant lounging
is an Art. THIS ART is Best practiced
with a willing Group of Friends, But can
Also be eAsily Applied to "people-you've-Just-
MeT-who-will-soon-Be-Friends."

WHen I started extravagantly lounging
with Friends, I reALized we were All
craving UNUSUAL AuThentic, vibrant
experiences we could share with our Friends.
This required A new vision and Description
and extravacant lounging WAS Born.

i enjoy lying
Down A lot in my life-
Some might say That I
LiVe Horizontally more
Than vertically.
it's Just so much
FuN
to lie DOWN with
Friends—
to lie About,
lounge Around,
elecently recline.
i think that
new THOUGHTS
spring From
relaxed
minds.

As I lounged with my friends, I noticed a very rich quality that was connected to our activities and conversations, and our friendships deepened. I named this activity "extravagant lounging" since I've always loved the LUSH connotations of the word "extravagant," and also because we save, conserve or ration in other areas of our lives, I think that we must be EXTRAVAGANT in our friendships.

extravagant not expensive

THESE extravagant lounging activities can take place anywhere friends can gather, and may contain a mixture of new and OLD things to do and ways to be TOGETHER.

MOST of us know how to lounge pretty well by ourselves. It takes some practice to lounge well with others. I'M including suggestions, "lounging ingredients" which you can use to inspire your own

EXTRAVAGANT LOUNGING

Good friends lie down happily and often

__I THINK__ THAT THE MAIN PURPOSE of extravagant lounging is to be with Friends in __new, meaning-full__ WAYS, and THis phrase and concept Awakens THis type of energy to be SHAReD.

__It's EASY__ To Become Hypnotized into Doing THe SAMe THings with our Friends, and THen wondering where

Deep enjoyment

went.

__I've DiscovereD__ THAT TAKING riSKs to connect Deeply with Friends is immensely

r e w A r d i n G

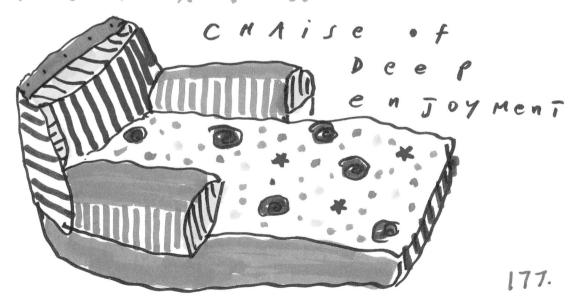

C H A i s e o f

D e e p

e n j o y m e n t

177.

I've also invited some of my succulent friends from "The Marvelous Message Board" to speak about their extravagant lounging experiences which often involve wearing PAJAMAS, TIARAS, BOAS or HATS together.

ALTHOUGH NONE of THAT is required

I wanted others to speak about their experiences, otherwise you might read this and think,

"Well, SARK is unusual, THAT'S WHY she can lounge about extravagantly, But it wouldn't work for me!"

These messages show that we can all lounge extravagantly.

Here's "DeNisey's" experience:

Imagine a shy woman who still feels like a little girl.
Imagine her going to a strangers house with a host of strangers, with the intent to prance around in jammies and boas!

Walking in the front door, greeted by cheers and feathers and glitter,
my heart jumped and I knew that this was going to be a lifelong memory of joy and belonging!

It was a freeing experience, one I repeated as often as possible. Going from the shy girl,
the one who taught a Salsa lesson at a Palooza and passed out Mardi Gras beads.

"In A Friend you Find A second self"
ISABelle Norton

178.

"Knoxy" Finds Support At A "Dangerous Tea"

After two months of posting, I ventured out to a Dangerous Tea in Los Angeles with several MMB members. It was all **women** – women who were open and sharing and growing and supportive. Women who I felt like I'd already known. Women who were **FUN** and I could actually be myself around! Women I could go to when I needed them! Holy Crap! And in LOS ANGELES... a place where I really doubted this stuff existed!!!

"S.G.Val" Glows in Radiant Company:

I spent the weekend with eight of the most amazing women I've ever met! They were *gorgeous*, *creative*, and *strong*! We shared our stories, made art together, talked about what we would do before we died. We soaked up the view in each others' presence from rocking chairs on a wooden porch with the most incredible view. We watched butterflies the size of my hand flutter around a huge bush outside the door – they were such fearless butterflies that we were able to get close enough to watch them eat and take great photographs. We adventured in the pouring rain and stumbled into a lesbian bar for shelter, where we enjoyed lush sofas and great drinks in a haven of women. We adventured more in that rain to the Mellow Mushroom, where we devoured delicious food, wild conversation, and laughed loudly.

We talked, we laughed often and loudly, joyously and honestly, we learned so much about each other, we drank and swore and shared deeply. We *GLOWED*!

extravagant lounging isn't only for women, and it doesn't even need to be extroverted or outrageous to "qualify."
Some of my deepest extravagant lounging has taken place by candlelight with very little talking and just being with friends.
When I set the stage for extravagant lounging, literally anything might take place, from:

"Promise me you'll always remember: you're braver than you believe, and stronger than you seem, and smarter than you think." A.A. Milne

179.

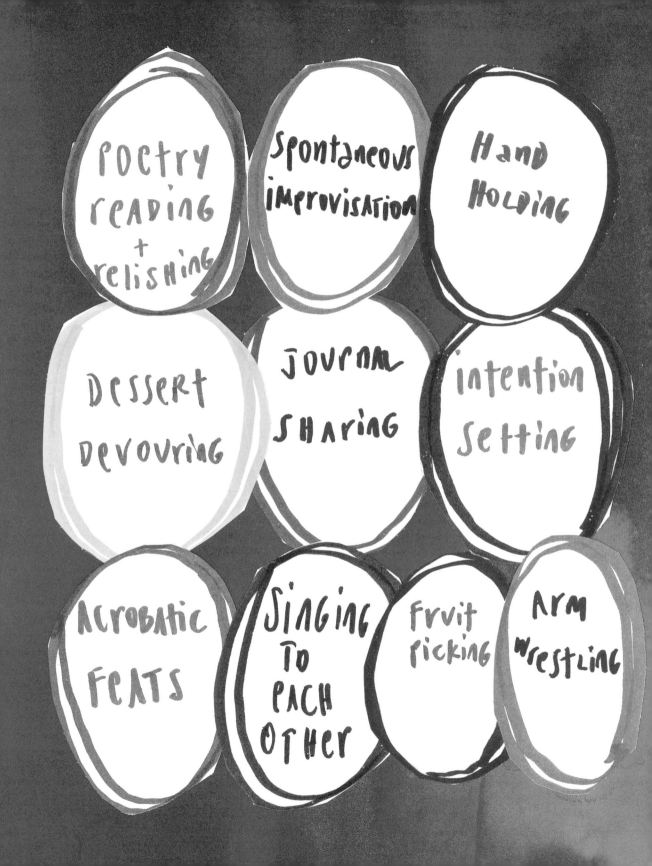

Your Guide to extravagant lounging with Friends

Your willingness to "Be comfortable" in the presence of other people. Some people need this encouragement, because they wonder "How it will look" if they're lying down in certain kinds of clothes

Wear lounging clothes! This could be pajamas or stretchy clothes that don't wrinkle. The most important ingredient is comfort. elastic works well.

Pick a spot Wherever lounging takes place, pick a spot that most appeals to you, and occupy it fully. You might bring along a robe or a blanket to make it even more comfortable.

let silences happen while lounging, there might be conversational lulls as people recline. This is "Filling the well" for the next words spoken.

Have no Agenda or expectation lounging defies rules or plans. It is enough to get together with Friends and lie around, doing nothing.

Horizontal causes wide thoughts

181.

FOOD, Wine, NAPS and "Doing nothing" with friends

PART OF THE ART of extravagant lounging is to be comfortable yourself while hosting such a gathering. Many hosts become tense or worried in advance, or are tired and crabby when the gathering occurs, especially if they've done "too much" to prepare. WHICH is common

Simplify

c   v   e   r   y   t   h   i   n   g

Preparation

I've reduced preparation to an hour or two at most. One of my favorite methods is something I call "BMLM," which stands for "Bare Minimum Last Minute" and is pronounced BIMLIM. It started after I discovered I wasn't having parties very often due to planning and preparation concerns.

remember to
relax...
it's the best gift
to a guest

182.

Here's my

"could be dinner and really isn't" menu for gatherings

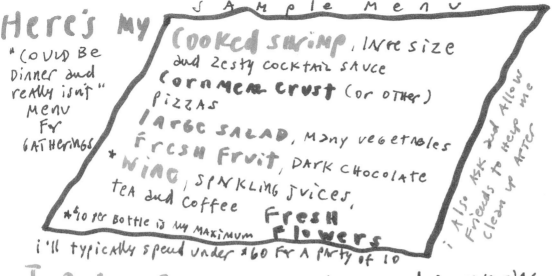

SAMPLE MENU

COOKED SHRIMP, large size and zesty cocktail sauce

CORNMEAL CRUST (or other) PIZZAS

large SALAD, many vegetables

FRESH FRUIT, dark chocolate

* WINE, SPARKLING JUICES, tea and coffee

FRESH FLOWERS

* $10 per bottle is my maximum

i also ask and allow friends to help me clean up after

i'll typically spend under $60 for a party of 10

I DELEGATE MUSIC, DRINKS and answering the DOOR, to other friends and spend my time talking with others about absolutely nothing.

THIS is one of my favorite ways to spend time with friends:

Doing "NOTHING"

with friends is a pleasurable ART and it needs encouragement. people often feel guilty if they're not "DOING SOMETHING".

Give them permission and a place to do NOTHING, and your friends will treasure your GATHERINGS. AND so will you.

THEN NAP HAPPILY AFTERWARDS

183.

FASCINATING CONVERSATIONS
WITH FRIENDS

YOUR FRIENDS Are FASCINATING. If you've FORGotten THAT, it's time for some new kinds of conversation Between you.

YOU Are FASCINATING

If you don't know THIS, Listen to me closely: It's A FACT, and an important trvTH ABOUT BeinG Your own Best Friend. we Are SO reADy To THINK THAT oThers Are FASCINATING, and ForGeT, or Don't know How To Bestow THose Blessings on ourselves.

You experience THose Blessings By PRACTICING Being FASCINATING, and THinking and Believing THAT you Are

FASCINATING CONVERSATIONS HAppen wHen

Friends Are curious, spontaneous, willing to play, interested in Themselves and oThers, and wHen we

STep out of THe ordinAry

and

risk

HAVing A More unusuAL conversATion

DO THis By introducing an uncommon topic or an ordinary topic seen in A new wAy. For exAmple,

184.

recently I met my brother's girlfriend for the first time, and asked each of them: "What do you like most about him or her?" I found out from her that my brother **glows** and **twinkles** when he looks at her — and we also had a fascinating conversation about the early stages of romantic relationships.

...melissa is a darling

My friend elissa and I discussed what makes a fascinating conversation, and then proceeded to have one about that very topic!

We leaned in over a candlelit table, and wove stories from past and present, asked each other thought-full questions and reflected on each other's answers.

A Giraffe Appeared on the table...

It's FASCINATING to hear new stories by old friends.

W e   c a n   T h i n k of ourselves as **FASCINATING** without being conceited, because they are quite simply unrelated.

You are fascinating and irresistible

BEGUILING
invitations
and how to extend them

Friends Adore being invited to anything and you can make beguiling invitations by utilizing a few easy creative suggestions:

- **Invent your own invitation** I used giant leaves to invite friends to a garden party. Use unusual fabrics, shapes, sizes or envelopes for your invitations.

- **Be clear** about what it is, where it is. Describe your gathering or party, what time it begins or ends, and specific directions if needed. This leaves people free to attend without calls or questions.

- **Send invitations** that you would like to receive. Think of favorite invitations you've received, and expand on the same theme, and do your own version.

- **Take a risk** Do your own invitations quickly or badly. Your friends will love the spontaneous quality!

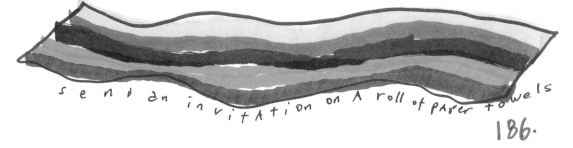

send an invitation on a roll of paper towels

186.

extravagant Lounging resources

THE JOY Diet
MARTHA BECK

SOUL FOOD CAFE
Dailywriting.net
A Truly extravagant place on the internet

Traveling Mercies
anne LAMOTT

Ten poems to change your Life
roger HOUSDEN

HALLELUJAH: The welcome TABle
MAYA Angelou

Live THE Life you Love
BARBRA SHer

THE invitation
OriAH

THE AMAZing power of Deliberate intent
esther and Jerry HickS (The Teachings of ABrAHAM)

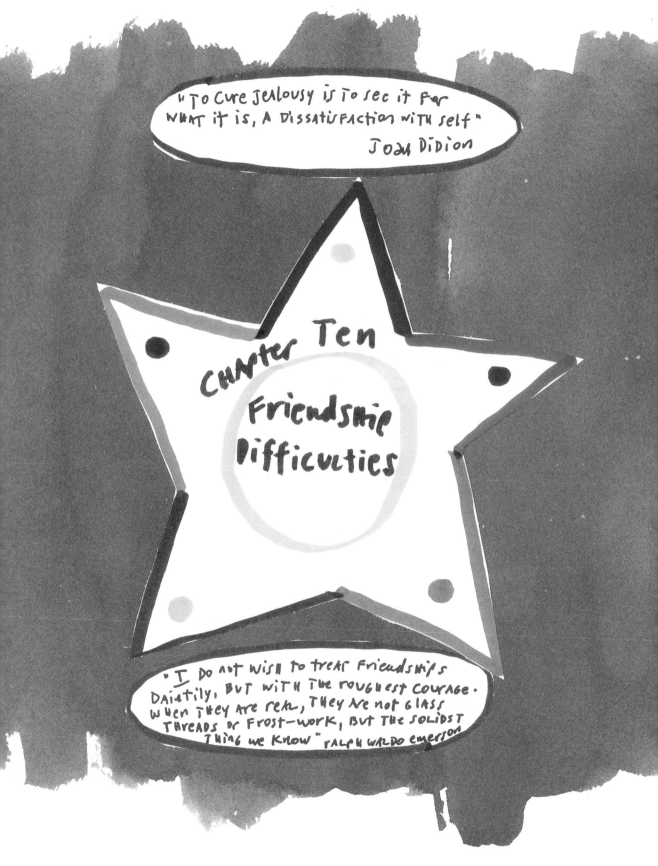

resentments and Grudges
in Friendships

Our Friendships will probably include upsets, conflict and unresolved issues. **It might sound lovely** to have Friendships be free of these issues, but they are part of our human learning curriculum.

When we don't experience resolution and clarity with conflicts in our Friendships, we often have resentments and Grudges. These kinds of feelings are often Hidden.

Hidden Feelings Cause Weight Gain

Friends can activate and trigger old wounds, and we have the choice whether to resent, withhold or manufacture resentments or grudge material because of this. We can also **choose** to communicate clearly, directly and compassionately.

I used to think that it was actually easier to hold resentments and grudges toward a friend than it was to tell the truth and clear it up.

This kind of negativity also impairs communications

"keep your friendship in repair"
—Ralph Waldo Emerson

We cannot experience deeper connections with a friend while ongoingly holding grudges and resentments.

It's easy to develop a habit of holding onto, or covering up grudges or resentments.

At first, they just seem too tiny to mention Then, more time goes by and it seems **silly** to bring the issue up. Or, life circumstances bring us bigger or more important content, and we "forget" the grudge or resentment.

This "forgetting" is not like letting go

I've feared that bringing up a resentment could damage a friendship. Sometimes it does, or appears to.

But usually that friendship was not strong or deep to begin with, and our truth-telling exposes its weakness.

Sometimes the friendship can change shape to adapt to these changes, sometimes **not.**

Some friendship clothes are just too small

192.

Sometimes THE BENEFITS OF GRUDGE HOLDING SEEMED to outweigh THE DISCOMFORT AND MESSINESS of **telling A Friend THE TRUTH.** Besides, I COULD "FORGET" THE GRUDGE and trick MYSELF into THINKING I WASN'T PRACTICING THIS BEHAVIOR

I WAS trained BY A MASTER GRUDGE HOLDER. MY MOTHER EXHIBITED relentless and HIGH-QUALITY GRUDGE HOLDING ABILITIES. **SHE frequently** explained and expressed THESE GRUDGES within THE FAMILY, BUT lied to THE people SHE HELD GRUDGES TOWARD.

This is very common

I remember ASKING Her ABOUT THIS BEHAVIOR, and SHE SAID,

"WELL, THEY DON'T KNOW I'm DOING THIS!"

I ASKED if it NEGATIVELY AFFECTED <u>HER</u> SINCE SHE KNEW SHE WAS HOLDING GRUDGES.

STACK
of
GRUDGES
STACKED
HIGH + teetering

193.

SHE MAINTAINED THAT it WAS no problem AT ALL. But I observed IHAT it WAS A PATTERN and HABit of negativity THAt Affected our WHole Family. It also caused me to Distrust Her. I didnt Always Believe WHAT SHe WOULD SAY to or ABout Her Friends, and relied instead on THE "Grudge report" THAT I Knew WOULD come lAter. SHe WOULD SAY,

"WELL, SHe doesnt ever invite me over, and Im just expected to continue issuing invitations."

I WOULD QUESTION Why SHe didnt just TALK to Her Friend Directly.

SHe WOULD respond,

"Friends dont Always understand, and it isnt worth THe trouble."

I WOULD silently wonder WHy THen we HAD to Hear ABout it.

My silence led to My own Grudges!

HOLDING resentments and Grudges towards Friends uses A tremendous Amount of energy.

194.

Consistently held grudges and resentments can wear at the fabric of a friendship, and make little tears in it.

AND SMALL BUMPS CAN BECOME BIG BUMPS

The more accumulated resentments and grudges, the more likely it is that a "big misunderstanding" can knock a friendship off it's foundations.

I've learned that:

- **It** isn't always necessary to admit a grudge or resentment to a friend directly. I can do my own work releasing it, and go forward in a new way with that friend.

- **I can have** open dialogues with close friends about grudges or resentments, and find them to be undisturbed & unafraid of what I've shared.

- **I can** communicate about these subjects sensitively, kindly and with compassion for myself and my friends.

"Certain flaws are necessary for the whole. It would seem strange if old friends lacked certain quirks." Goethe

195.

- **I need to** time these kinds of communications appropriately.

- **I can become aware** when or if I'm slipping into an old habit or pattern.

- **I can experience** or express a resentment or grudge, and find it to be humorous.

- **I can recognize** that I'm inclined towards holding on rather than letting go, and allow for that in my friendships.
  I can also see that I'm always changing, and so are my friends

- **I can be** braver at revealing what I'm really thinking and feeling with friends.

- **I can transform** resentments into opportunities for truth, and choose not to carry resentments or grudges.

I can be present to hear a friend's grudges and resentments toward me, and not take them personally.
and it's a challenge to do!

I can live my friendship life largely free of these patterns.

I can sometimes hold grudges or resentments and still be a good friend to myself and others.

I can swiftly release grudges and resentments.

I've learned *i'll be practicing* these lessons and am practicing new behaviors, by *mostly* doing the **opposite** of every item on this list. **I falter and stumble,** tell lies and avoid conflict, in order to "keep the friendship." Then I remember that **telling my truth** is what **nourishes** my self-friendship, and allows me to experience all of my fabulous friendships fully.

especially when they sometimes don't feel so fabulous

Jealous Feelings in Friendships

Feeling Jealous of a friend is common, yet less commonly spoken of or acknowledged. We would all like to just "**Be Happy**" for whatever good things happen to a friend, but the truth is, sometimes we feel jealous.

My Jealous Feelings seem to arise during times of insecurity, or when I'm feeling much younger than my chronological age, so I've learned to take this into account and allow for it. **It's uncomfortable** writing about jealous feelings, especially any jealous feelings towards friends. I frequently think that I should be "**Better Than This**" or above it in some way. I also feel **embarrassed** sometimes to even have these feelings. **When I feel jealous, I** also often feel ashamed. **The feelings** just wash over me like some kind of strange heat. **Sometimes** I'll have outbursts and just exclaim out loud to a friend that I feel jealous.

This often eases the pressure and the feelings can dissolve

198.

Sometimes the friend and I can just laugh about it, or discuss it. I've learned that whatever I feel jealous of is usually something I'd like for myself, so I take it as a signal to begin exploring how to have that experience too.

Here's what I've discovered about my outer-directed jealous feelings:

* **Jealous** feelings are not rational.
* **They're** usually not as solid & strong as they first appear.
* **They** come from some unexplored or untended area in myself.
* **They** can be communicated, clarified, explored and put to rest.

Here are a few of my recent jealousies

Marney's Good hiring abilities

Val's basketball skills and great jeans

McNair's art journals

Joshua's exercise routine

anyone that can type fast

Andrew's ability to ignore things

people who have or adopt babies and appear to live happily and easily with them

199.

I'M ALSO the recipient of friend's jealous feelings towards me, and have noticed how I respond when that happens. **I usually feel** uncomfortable and sometimes want to give that friend whatever they think they're lacking, because I can exquisitely relate to their jealous feelings. and sometimes feel guilty for what I have

I HAVE ALSO at times, minimized my own good news, in order to avoid the possibility of a jealous response.

i don't recommend doing this — it doesn't work!

MOST times I can just observe how it feels to have someone be jealous of me, and not try to manage or take care of their experience.

As a recipient of others' jealous feelings, I've discovered:

I'M not responsible for other people's feelings.

It does no good to try to diminish or minimize my experience so "they" don't feel jealous.

Other people's feelings really have nothing to do with me.

Most of all, I believe that jealous feelings need to flow — whatever those 200.

Feelings Are.

The f l o w i n g might
take place in journaling, conversations
with close friends, a therapist, or healing
conversations with the self. There are
times to admit and discuss jealous feelings
with friends, and there are times to work
through those feelings privately.

I've recently learned that admitting jealousy
to a friend can be made more complicated
by their reaction. It can activate a friend
focusing on what you told them about your jealous
feelings, **even after you've gotten over it.**

A friend might say;

"Oh that's right, this made you jealous
before. Is it okay if I talk about it?"

I've learned that when I share my jealous
feelings with a friend, I must also add that
I don't need to be taken care of in the future
about it by them altering their behavior or
what they tell me — mostly I just need to
be heard and acknowledged.

201.

On my journey, it's been fascinating sharing jealous feelings with friends and finding out what they feel or have felt jealous of, with me. I've learned that we're all jealous sometimes, and it doesn't need to be a **Hidden subject.**

Jealous feelings can be a valuable tutor about where we're experiencing lack or insecurity in some way

We can Heal any lack or insecurity by allowing jealous feelings to **Flow** and show us what it is we might be wanting.

Here are some Questions to ask yourself:

- **Are** you ever jealous and don't express it? Why or why not?

- **Have** you expressed jealousy and gotten a negative response? If so, how has this affected you?

- **Have** you experienced others' jealousy of you? If so, how has this affected you?

- **Can** you envision being more open about your jealous feelings? Why or why not?

WAYS TO respond to negative friends

AS FRIENDS, we all witness each other's negative moods or habits, and times of fear and not-knowing. When we can TRULY HEAR A friend complain, vent or just speak about what HURTS, we can provide a safe space for their feelings, and of course, they can do the same for us when we need it. But, there is another type of behavior friends might engage in, which I'm calling "repetitive attitude of negativity."

THIS is where a friend complains and TALKS ABOUT WHAT HURTS, without owning their own experience.

it's clear that nothing you say helps, nor does the listening itself help

WHEN ENGAGED in this behavior, a friend often cannot see what they're doing. They will repetitiously recirculate negative energy, and you'll notice that you'll feel drained during or after you've spent time with them.

203.

It's exhausting to hear someone endlessly complain, find the worst thing in each situation, and then repeat. **We all do this occasionally.**

I'm talking about the friend who does this consistently. It might sound something like this:

"**Oh** we'll never find parking. Last time I was here, I looked for over an hour."

"**I'm sure** They won't _____. Last time They didn't _____."

"**I know** we'll never _____. Last time They said no."

"Last time" becomes the mantra, which doesn't help us in the **N O W.**

It isn't just **unpleasant** to be around a friend who's repetitively negative; **it's toxic.** By tolerating this behavior, you're encouraging your friend to be toxic.

204.

Here's WHAT you can DO To protect yourself and HELP your Friend WHo is stuck in THESE HABits:

*remember THAT repetitive Attitudes of negativity Are not Healed By someone Listening, But By someone TRUTH Telling

- **Center** yourself By Deep BreATHing, or By visuALizing Being Grounded Through The Bottoms of your feet into The Center of THe eArTH.

- **SPeAK** Kindly and Directly to your Friend ABout Their Attitude and BeHavior and How it Affects you. This can reALly HeLP sHift The energy, and MAKe THem AWARe.

- **respond** CALMly By ASKing A few Questions THAT Can Assist your Friend in Getting to A More neutral place

- **See** if you can Help offer other outlets For your Friend to express WHAT THey're Feeling, and remind THem THAT you love and cAre ABout THem.

- **If** THey're not reAdy or willing to cHange, you can Decide How MucH Time you can, or will spend Time with This friend.

It is A Friendship GiFT to HeLP A Friend out of A BAD HABit

If you Are THe one exHibiting repetitive Attitudes of negativity, Become AWAre of THis HABit and ASK A Good Friend to Help you By pointing out (Gently) WHen you're Doing it.

Friendship Difficulties resources

Friends
Witness
Sadness
and
Catch
Tears
with
Tenderness

When There Are Conflicts

Which Are Different From Hurts, resentments or jealousies. We all experience conflict in friendships Because we're all Different

Friendships Are Gifts, not Obligations

I'm still learning this one. It is easy to have a mental list of "requirements" for a friend to fulfill. You might think;

My Friend Should,

"**Be** Sympathetic whenever I'm sick."

"**Be** Aware when I'm going through something difficult and check on me."

"**Be** Able to stop telling her own story sometimes and listen to mine."

"**Be** willing to initiate Fun Activities At least As much As I do."

It is much more difficult to unconditionally love and learn from our friendships. Most of us "keep score" with our Friends, even though we say we don't.

"**if** He Doesn't Call Back, I'm **not** Calling Him. He Always Does this! I'm Always the one to Call First."

"Value friendship for what there is in it, not for what can be gotten out of it"
— H. Clay Trumbull

209.

In the curious alchemy THAT MAKES UP our friendships, we can forget THAT our differences fill us as much as our similarities. Of course, we search for those connections and similarities.

"Look! She likes spending time in bookstores too." But as a friendship grows and deepens, it is the differences that challenge and sustain us. We learn THAT when we are ragged or desperate or disagreeable and friends still love us, we can then see ourselves with more loving eyes. The differences teach us to be tolerant and loving even when we disagree.

Most of us have not learned to have conflicts with a friend and keep our connection. If we do fight, we often do it covertly, usually by telling another friend:

"Can you believe WHAT he did? I'll never count on him for that again."

If we DO tell a friend directly what hurt or angered us, their response is usually then fed through our filter of "what friends say or don't say" to each other. If their response fits our filter, then we can process our feelings.

210.

If Their response doesn't Fit, we often turn away from THAT particular Friendship.

Many of us try to avoid conflict altogether By anticipating areas of disagreement and not discussing Them. By **CHANGING** what we say or Think so we don't upset a friend, or By Hiding certain Differences From each other.

we Hide who we are

If we successfully avoid areas of conflict, Then we Think we can just "enjoy The friendship." We Forget, or Don't realize, That conflict (is) a part of The friendship, and THAT when we can open ourselves to whatever feelings arise, we Deepen our connection and our ability to have an intimate, authentic friendship.

When we spend close, intimate Time with Friends, we will probably notice certain "unfriendly" feelings within ourselves;

"I didn't realize He was such a Bad Driver!"

"How can she possibly Forget Her purse when it's Time to pay The check?"

"I Hate How oblivious she seems to My Feelings."

211.

WE COUNT on our Friendships in significant ways, and are Deeply Affected by their changes and absences.

I LOST a good Friend around the same time my mother died, and this loss hurt almost as much as the death of my mother. **BOTH of US** tried to talk about the lost friendship, and ultimately couldnt understand what had happened. **eventually,** we just gave up trying to talk about it, and the friendship ended.

UNLiKE love relationships, I think it is common for friendships not to have closure. It is more likely that changed friendships just FADE Away or disappear. I dont think that the **Friendship** itself disappears, I think that our willingness to decipher and process the feelings of that relationship does. There are friendships that just fade with time and distance, of course. Most of us have experienced this.

212.

"Between Friends there is no need of justice." Aristotle

A college friend becomes a once-a-year holiday card friend, and if the cards stop, we don't continue the friendship. It can just feel too difficult to reestablish feelings of friendship. OR, we reach out to connect and find that the friendship feels forced or false.

THE GIFTS of friendship are found in all of these changes. even when friendships fade or end, the friendship is still part of us—it has contributed to HOW WE ARE IN THE WORLD, WHO WE ARE AS friends.

EVERY HURT experienced in friendship is a perfect teacher for our "unconditional loving class of life." PART of friendships is THE HURT. WHAT WE CHOOSE TO DO WITH THAT PAIN is PART of our lessons in friendship.

"THE WORLD is round and the place which may seem like the end may also be the beginning."
—Ivy Baker Priest

213.

Silences in Friendships

I've been a previous master at silences with friends. When there was conflict or pain, my way of dealing with it was to disappear or be silent.

i thought that silence would mend the pain.

WHAT I discovered instead was that I was actually

A V O I D I N G   perceived p a i n.

I've learned that there were high costs to my avoiding habit. The highest cost was

A B s e n c e   o f   L o v e.

When I'm busy avoiding, I'm basically blocking love.

After conflicts with friends, I sometimes "freeze" people in place, where we last talked, what we last said, or what they said. In my mind I would go over and over the insult, or the sentence that

HURT the MOST. I'd ALMOST PUT A FRAME
Around it and HANG it up!
This "Freezing" people
in place could go on
for years, leading to
long silences.
Recently I experienced
A revelation About this. I'd

NEGATIVE THOUGHTS Don't DESERVE GOOD FRAMES

HAD A tough ending with A good friend A
number of years Ago, and we'd finally been Able
to TALK enough About what happened to reclaim
the love and HAVE A kind of Distant Friendship.

    We Also talked About what it would
TAKe to go from Distant Friends to closer
Friends. She said,

    "It just feels like it would take so
Much time and energy to process what
Happened before, and who has the time and
energy for that? I don't think I do."

    I Heartily Agreed, and Also felt
secretly relieved, because my other

GUIDING LIGHT (Besides Avoidance of pAin) HAS Been,

Avoidance of further pAin

It seemed to me THAT if we HAD some "BiG tALK," it couLD AlL GET worse, MisunderstandinGs couLD Develop, and we couLD end up BeinG even less close THan we Are riGHT now!

Of course, WHen I'm ThinKinG Like this, THere's no cHance THAT ThinGs can Get Better As A result of TALKinG.

So I carried THAT sentence Around in My HEAD For MONTHs:

"It FeeLs Like it nouLD TAKe too MUCH Time and enerGy."

And Froze My Friend in place, sAyinG This sentence over and over in My MinD.

My MinD sometimes GeTs stuck.

216.

JUST the OTHER DAY, THIS Friend
CAlled and suggested A spontaneous TALK
and visit— in 5 Minutes time.
She lives out of town, so I didn't expect the call at all

My immediate internal response
WAS an AUTOMATIC NO, WHICH I've learned
not to trust until I ASK;
"WHAT'S MY MOST ALIVE CHOICE?"
The answer WAS immediate.
"See Her."
As we tALKed, I reflected THAT sHe
HAD said THAT sentence ABout not HAVING The
Time and energy to process our Difficulties.
SHe responded,
"I said THAT? THAT's stupid. I think
We could HAVe just one conversation
and clear just ABout anyThing up."
In THAT split second, I realized
THAT sHe HAD CHanGed After sAYing THAT
sentence, MonTHs Before. I HAD "Frozen" Her.

WE ARE ALL CHANGING, ALL THE TIME.
EACH of us is free to CHANGE, GROW
and revisit anything THAT HAS BEEN SAID
or DONE. WE ARE not FROZEN or "locked
in" or "convicted" For THINGS WE SAID.

   I want to experience MYSELF and
EACH Friend AS A MULTidimensional
CHANGING, Growing SOUL, CAPABLE of BEING
new in EACH Moment.

   I can Question WHAT MY friend said
Before, and revisit it LATER.

   I can DisAgree with WHAT MY Friend
SAYS, and still Be friends or not.

   I can Modify or CHANGE MY reActions
to friends without needing silence or
Avoidance.

   I can respond Non-HABitually By
CHOOSING COMMUNICATION over silence.

   I can realize THAT pAin Does not
necessarily Dissolve THROUGH silence.

                              218.

I can KNOW THAT consciously and carefully chosen silences can teach and heal in certain friendship situations.
THE BALM of no words

I've Also learned THAT pain can Actually multiply through silence. Misunderstandings can grow and the climate of silence leaves room for the MAGNIFICATION of pain.

in silence, There is The illusion of no Further pain

I WATCHED my Mother practice This Behavior. She maintained silences for years and Then recounted Her "evidence" THAT justified The silence. The evidence was always something Hurtful THAT HAD Been mentally frozen By Her, and was now Being recounted, As if it HAD JUST HAppened. She endlessly recycled The stories of WHAT HAD HuRT Her, repeating The insults word for word, As Though They were precious and MUST Be remembered.

219.

I I think we can forget that love and friendships are precious.

How many times do we remember and recount tender, beautiful things a friend has done or said?

I was at a party just after having these new awarenesses, and noticed how often people recount insults or injustices. I just walked away from those conversations. I don't want to spend my precious friendship time practicing that old habit anymore, of repeating pain, and punishing friends and myself, through unconscious silences.

I plan on turning my silences now into nourishment and not punishment and offering communication.

220.

anger
in Friendships

MOST of the friendships I've lost or chosen not to continue were affected by my fear and avoidance of anger— mine or theirs, it didn't really matter.

If anger was a component, I wanted out. **NOW** I'm very aware that anger is just an energetic emotion, and valuable for my friendships. I can now become **AWARE** of my anger, feel it, and express or communicate it much more directly.

I've included anger in my emotional range. Sometimes I feel angry with my friends, and they with me. **Sometimes** we process through anger together, sometimes it's work I do on my own.
Sometimes I just hide from anger still

THERE'S A MARVELOUS BOOK called "The rule of Two: observations on close relationship" by Ann Woodin with Drawings by Andrew Rush.

221.

"**WITHOUT A DOUBT,** unexpressed and unreceived Thank-yous and resentments leaves Holes in THE FABRIC of relationship, and soon It Becomes A rather Breezy AFFAIR. It WOULD HARDLY keep A BABY rABBiT WARM."

FROM "The Rule of Two"
By ann woodin

WHen anger Gets stuck Between Friends, it can leAD To The loss of THAT Friendship, and even years of pAin. My Avoidance of anger Used to Be so complete THAT I didit even Allow Myself to FeeL angry.

Holes in relationship FAbric

THen when I Accepted it, I still FeLt angry A lot of The Time.

NOW anger comes and Goes WiTH Friends and I dont pAY so MuCH Attention to it.

It isnt Always necessAry to process anger with friends. It can Be enough to ACKnowledge it, Feel it, and let it GO.

222.

IN THE BOOK, ann describes a
process that I've used very effectively:

Just read through or write down answers after you
recall an upset with a friend, or when you felt angry

1. exactly when did you first become upset?

2. What are your complaints/accusations?

3. What are your feelings?

4. What are your reasons and justifications
for your complaints?

5. What are your expectations?

Complete the following sentence:

If only she/he would _____

_____ Then I would _____

_____.

Should he/she suddenly appear before your
eyes would you feel

warm and loving ☐   upset ☐

If your answer is "upset," in all likelihood
you are holding onto the point of view, "it's
her fault," which you are reinforcing with
your reasons. every point of view has
attached to it a benefit and a cost.

223.

Our tendency to HOLD our anger and freeze the situation keeps anger stuck and current.

Part of letting GO means allowing our anger to MELT through expression or just a bit of attention. This attention might take the form of a phone call, a letter, or some journaling about your anger and what you're angry about.

"You see somebody that you've known, and you think they are continuous. You think they are one whole thing, but the truth is that they are a GREAT SWARM of processes holding themselves in equilibrium, and at various times in their lives, they may assume ideas, positions that are the opposite of what they thought before, but they are the same person."

Diane Ackerman
from CULTIVATING DELIGHT: A NATURAL HISTORY OF MY GARDEN

224.

"If you're going through hell, keep going" Winston Churchill

FORGiveness WiTH Friends
and WiTH ourselves

"Forgiveness means to Give up
resentment or THe Desire to punish.
our principal Job on eARTH is To
Forgive."

From "THe rule of Two" By ann woodin

For. Giving is truly an "inside Job."
Forgiveness Does **NOT** mean THAT THe Hurting
Actions or PAtterns Are Allowed to continue.

Forgiveness is a release and a relief.
It is Also A process THAT HAppens in layers,
not in A linear progression.

I've studied Forgiveness and practiced
fr yeNrs, since I uncovered THAt I'd Been
sexually and physically Abused By A FAmily
member. I WAS convinced THAt I would
never Forgive. I didnt Forgive The Actions;
I Forgave THe person, and THAt Forgiveness
work continues. Forgiving Friends HAS BOTH
Been BOTH easier and more Difficult to learn.
easier when THe Actions Are smaller, more Difficult

WHEN I HAVE trouble REALIZING THAT Forgiveness is needed.

Forgiving myself HAS Been THe Most Difficult Of All. Releasing self-judgment HAS Been Pivotal work for Me, and I'm continually learning How to Forgive Myself.

I recommend A BOOK Called "Forgive for Good" By Dr. Fred Luskin, WHO I Believe HAS BROVGHT THe Mind and BODY TOGETHer For Forgiveness Work. He Teaches BreaTHing and Meditation exercises to Allow you to step out of any intellectual understanding of Forgiveness, and into THe Heart of it. One of His concepts Has Helped me tremendously ALSO: THe ideA THAT you Are Like an Air traffic controller, and UNForgiven THings Are Like planes Filling The SKY.

It takes a lot of energy to keep track of those planes, and Monitor Their progress and Activities. Dr. Luskin says:

"AND THROUGHOUT All eternity, I Forgive you, you Forgive me"
William BLAKe

"you Must let Those planes land. Let Them land."

Once I Began practicing "letting those planes land," and learning to integrate My Mind and BODY with regard to Forgiveness, By practicing The exercises in Dr. Luskins Book, I've Been Able to Forgive Myself and My Friends More consistently.

226.

When Friendships Hurt resources

When Friendship HURTS
Jan Yager PH.d.

Fearless Living
Rhonda Britten

THE DARK Side of THE LIGHT CHASERS
Debbie Ford

cnvc.com
Non-violent Communication Skill Teachings

WHen THE HEART WAits
Sve Monk Kidd

Letting Go of THE Person you used to Be
LAMA SuryA DAS

Centering and THE Art of intimacy
Gay Hendricks Ph.d. KATHLyN Hendricks Ph.d.

Transitions
Julia CAMeron

"Friendship demands the ability to do without it"
RALPH WALDO EMERSON

Chapter Twelve

Managing Time and energy in Friendships

"The fun is having friends who help each other get free"
RAM DASS

WHen To extend yourself To Friends and For WHAT

Recently A Friend Asked For HELP DVring A MOVE, and I WAS in THe Middle of writing THis BOOK and concerned About Being ABle to HELP HER and still Get my work Done. I started to tell Her I wouldnt Be ABle to HELP, and THen reaLized it WAS More of my "All or NOTHing" THinking:

"eiTHer I'll HELP THe MOST, or I won't HELP AT All."

I WAS THe "Hero" in my BiologicAL FAmily. THis MeAns I've Gotten A lot out of rescuing, SAVing, Being the "One WHO HELPS THe MOST." Since THAT Gets exHAusting, my oTher WAy is to not Do any THing to HELP. BOTH WAYS of THinking Are not nourishing to myself or Friends, and I'm leArning A lot ABout practicing A "Middle WAY" WHere I DO WHAT I can For Friends, in A HEALTHy SELF-nourishing WAY.

So I decided to help my friend for an hour or two and packed some boxes, talked about some solutions for things, and did the dishes. I left and returned to my writing without feeling t i r e d, **overwhelmed** or that I'd done "too much." But, I also wondered if I'd helped "enough."

Later, my friend told me how grateful she was for my help, how glad she was just to see me, and that she'd called some other friends to help her further.

This experience was a tremendous shift for me. I saw that I could extend myself without overextending — that my friendship assistance had been valuable for her and healthy for me.

I actually felt puzzled that my help had been "enough" because in my mind previously,

nothing was ever enough!

and to that part of my mind, nothing ever will be

231.

Of course, none of my friends HAD expected me to over function or overextend. I'd BeHaved This way in line with my previous conditioning growing up. and of course, my Friends Are subject to THeir conditioning!

As The "Hero," I'd Gotten A lot of Attention, Accolades and conditional Approval. This **served** to Feed my eGo and Set up "conditional loving" in my relationships.

WiTH regard to my Friendships, I HAD THOUGHT it MADe me More VAluABle or loved, or A Better Friend to Be This "Hero." Of course, we can't "**B u y**" our Friendships with This type of BeHavior. Friends may experience DisAppointMent if we're not ABle to Help AS MUCH AS THey'd Hoped, But ULtimAtely Friendship is A GiFT and noT an oBLiGATion.

I'd like to suggest something I invented called THE "FAVOR CLUB." It works well for long-term close friendships.

Here's how it can work. A friend asks you to babysit for 3 to 4 hours. You willingly say yes, and apply those hours to the FAVOR CLUB ACCOUNT — you can use a notebook or set something up online. Then, you can ask for help from them, and "subtract" from the account.

For example, my friends VAL and CLARK sometimes ask me to take care of their son JONAH, which I love doing. Sometimes I need help with my computer and one of them helps me.

it's not necessary for us to keep an actual "account"

We keep loose track of this in our minds and feel more confident and happy asking for or receiving help.

works well in friendships

233.

So many if us Are comfortABle GiViNG to our Friends, and MUCH less FAMiliN WiTH **Receiving**— so THE FAVor cluB works As an incentive for GiViNG _and_ receiving.

Some people AlreaDy Do THis kind of THiNG withovt DiscussiNG it out loud. **Friends** operAte with All sorts of UnspoKen codes v contrACTS wiTH eACH oTHer.

<u>I</u> THink it's Fun and interestiNG To nAme and speAK ovt loud WHAT we **WiSH** For or tope for in our Friendships.

It HeLps us leArn and Grow in THis reGArd. **We can learn** to exteud Ourselves to our Friends in positive ways THAT FeeL Good and **Receive** similAr BeneFit in return.

Most of us Are AFrAid to sAy NO Directly To A Friend, and will insteAD

AVOid or tell Little lies, To not lose The connection or LOVE.
We FORGET THAT Friendship is Meant to nowish and not Deplete us.
We FORGET to tAke cAre of ourselves FirsT Before we exteud to A Friend.

THiS MeanS THAT we exQuisiteLy prActice HiGH-QuALity self-cAre For ourselves, and only THen HeLp A Friend.

USe THe HeLpiNG eNerGy wisely

235.

"Let's get Together and Catch up:" Let's not

Sometimes I don't call or contact friends because of this concept of "catching up." If I haven't spoken with a friend for many months or even years, it just feels like too much work to "catch up." It feels like we'll need to communicate for countless hours just to get caught up to where we are now!

I understand that it's just a phrase, and the intention behind it is good, but it causes me to sometimes **not connect** with friends if it's been a while.

I propose that we drop this phrase and concept, and just realize that if we communicate with our friend, we'll just naturally find out how they are, and what's been going on with them.

I'm going to release myself from

any pressure to "CATCH up," and CALL THose FrienDs I've Been AVoiding and suggest THAT we just start From How we Are N O W and GO BACKWARDS From THere if we want to.

Also, "CATCHing up" implies THAT we HAVe FALLen BeHind someHow, and I don't Believe THAT TIme is THAT lineAr. It isn't just About A progression of events Along A certAin TIme line, But A MVLti-lAyered AffAir, with telepATHic AwAreNesses THrown in.

WHAT we or our frieNds HAVe Been DOING in THe time we didn't communicATe is less important THan our BEING or essence, and THAT you can only Discover THrovGH Being present WITH A FrieNd.

expectations of friends

There's a saying in the BAHAMAS and JAMAICA that I often heard when I lived there:

"THAT'S JUST THE WAY SHE GO."

It was usually followed by a shrug of the shoulders. It's used to describe how someone typically behaves, even if it's ODD or anti-social.

I experienced it as a marvelous statement of Acceptance of the sometimes unusual ways friends act. It's common to form expectations of friends, based on past behavior and self-interest.

"OH, he always calls if he's going to be late."

"OH, she would never do THAT."

" I can always count on _____,
    for _____."

We all participate in this "expectation system."

238.

WE MIGHT set ourselves up with high expectations and then continually experience disappointment if changes with friends occur. OR, we try not to have any expectations AT ALL, and then we feel like we're lying to ourselves. PERHAPS we have moderate expectations and ADJUST them accordingly to each individual friendship.

EXPECTATIONS of ourselves and our friends can take a variety of forms. MOST of us have a "code of conduct" of some kind for our friends THAT we carry around inside our HEAD, either from experience or from WHAT we were TAUGHT.

Friendship Code of Conduct

Friends always ———————.
Friends never ———————.
If you want to be a good friend, you need to ——————— and ———————.

SOME of THESE expectations are noble or generous, but some are connected to a PAYBACK of some kind.

239.

For example: "I expect that we will share sad times, and that I'll be very involved if my friend experiences a death in her family."

Then, my friend will be sure to help me later

Then, when we experience a death in our family, we might expect a friend to be present and involved.

This was my expectation with a former close friend who disappeared from my life during my mother's health decline and eventual death. I expected that she would be there for me, and she wasn't. I tried to contact her a number of times and she wouldn't respond.

and i knew she had received the messages

I felt so sad and angry and cheated out of my expectation, and hurt by my friend. Yet our friendship had changed, and we were no longer speaking. Obviously my friend couldn't deal with me or my mother's death.

240.

WHY HADNt I ADJusted My expectAtions?

I clung to the expectAtions THAT HAD Formed over A long Friendship, and then didnt reADjust As THAT Friendship chAnged over Time.

Certainly There Are "reAsonAble" expectAtions For Friendships:

- reciprocity
- COMMONALity
- Some degree of sAfety
- Time spent or shAred

But The Degree of expectAtion For everything in Friendship is inDIVidual, and can Be chAnged or shifted As THE Friendship Grows or chAnges.

we can
ADJust
our
Vision

241.

We can:

- **look closely** AT our expectations in our friendships and Be More Aware of WHAT THey MiGHT Be

- **explore** WHAT we expect of Ourselves As Friends, and ADJUST THAT As needed

- **Learn** WHETHer We HAVE HIGH, Low or Medium expectations and how THAT Affects our Friendships

- **Discuss** with Friends our Mutual expectations and whether They Are current or relevant

Tailoring our expectations creates honesty and Mutual respect, which is The FOUNDATION of every strong Friendship.

Friendships Are like waves and sometimes we wave Goodbye!

Canceling or Changing plans with friends without negative consequences

I'M KNOWN By My friends as the "Queen of changed plans." They MARVEL at How often and easily I change plans, and some of my friends Have Adopted These Practices for Themselves, since Being friends with me.

It all started when I realized How often I WAS engaged in planned Activities with friends THAT didn't feel nourishing or Satisfying. Later I would check in with My friend and find out THAT They HADn't really enjoyed The plan either. We were clearly Being "tyrannized By plans."

Most of us MAKe plans with friends in order to Have fun or connect, and Then feel nervous or cautious About changing a plan THAT isn't, or Doesn't Actually provide, fun.

243.

Of course There Are Social Occasions when plans may need to be kept. But for Getting together with friends, I use a looser system. **My friend Val** calls it "Mood Based" since it is dependent on The mood I'm in at The time, and the mood of my friend. But I Also call it The "**Beauty of The Tentative plan.**" With willing friends, This is How it works: **We choose** A mutually Satisfying date, and check in That day To see what our moods and energies are Like, and adjust The plan accordingly. This system works Best when Both people Are willing To Be Flexible and spontaneous

Then if either friend wants To Change The plan or cancel it for any reason, or without reason, There Are no consequences Like **Guilt** or other Bad Feelings and Best of All, There Are no lies. This system Also promotes

Spontaneous JOY, since

Many GreAT Things Are Discovered serendipitously or By "Accident" and if A "plan" is ADHered to, THAT GreAT experience MAY Be Missed.

Another Benefit of This system is more chances to spend time with Friends, since we're often reluctant to Make plans During BUSY or stressful Times, The BeAuty of The tentative plan promotes more possibilities to Actually GeT TogeTHer, since we know we can CHange or cancel AT The lAsT Minute.

It's eAsy To Discuss This with Friends and AGree which plans need A Bit More commitment, and which will Benefit From A looser system.

i will tenderly ADMit A contrADiction in Myself: THAT even I sometimes would Like to HAve A More committed plan and don't Always Ask for it, and Then Feel sAD or A Bit HurT when A Friend Gleefully CHanges or cancels The plan

it's The ugliness of The tentative plan

245.

THen THere Are THe GiFts of canceling A plan with Friends. I started checking with friends After needing to cancel, and found out THAT THe MAJority of THe Time, My Friend FELT SO GLAD For THe unexpected Time. It's AS THOUGH THAT kind of Time TAKes on A SPECIAL GLOW Because it WAS unexpected.

Since we sHAre Time with Our Friends, and we're All Different Types of people, I Believe There's A lot More room For More kinds of planning styles.

I've identified Some of My Friends As "Long-term planners," and we compromise when planning together. Other Friends Are SO Mood-BAsed, we rarely get Together Because neither of us wants to commit to A plan.

246.

Many of my friends and I happily change and cancel without negative consequences, and have discussed how we feel about this subject ahead of time, so that our respective friendship needs are also being met.

This method of focusing on individual planning styles removes conflict about plans between friends. We are then free to experience more joy-full connection in our friendships.

PART THREE

integration

A self-proclamation

Friendships Are our real "trust funds." We can trust in their consistency, even as they shift and change. As GERALD JAMPOLSKY says in "Love is letting go of Fear,"

"The arms from which you've come to expect love may change, but the Love itself will never change."

We can trust that our friendships will continue all of our lives, and that our primary friendship with ourselves will grow stronger and more flexible (with practice) and even more fulfilling with time. To able to fully experience this, I recommend

THIS SELF-PROCLAMATION

AS I Age and change, I intend to make and have Friends of All Ages and kinds

MAY My Judgments and criticisms soften

MAY My expectations of friends dissolve to make more room for unconditional Friendships

MAY I rest Happily in the Arms of Loving Friends

MAY I continue practicing fighting with Friends As fiercely and Fairly As is needed

MAY I continue to untangle past conditioning from present Friendships

MAY I love My Friendship with Myself As keenly and clearly As I do My other Friendships

MAY I Be A truth-teller, truth receiver and wise Friend

MAY I invest fully in my Friendships without counting what comes back

Our Fabulous Friendships
and what they give to us

There are so many fabulous books about friendships. However, I noticed an absence of books about **BOTH** celebrations and challenges. **And the truth is**, our friendships are a **messy blend** of both.

Friendships are dynamic, ever-changing entities, and we outgrow certain friendships or aspects of ourselves in those friendships, all of our lives.

Our ability to integrate the celebrations and challenges is directly related to our practicing **allowing, acknowledging** and **accommodating** all the aspects of ourselves and of our friends. The more we're able to do this, the more we'll be able to receive from our friendships. **In order** to experience friendship integration, we must be willing to **say unpopular things, hear** reflections of ourselves that aren't always attractive, and get into and out of conflicts regularly. 250.

integration practice

integration practice includes:

- **Being** aware of our faults and flaws and how they impact our friends
- **Witnessing** a friend's faults and flaws without distancing in the friendship
- **Being** able to ask for and receive support, even when we're more comfortable doing it ourselves
- **Offering** and receiving unconditional love, even when we feel full of conditions
- **Telling** the truth even when it's painful, uncomfortable or it seems like we could get away with lying
- **Living** at a "higher vibration" in our friendships—this means looking with loving eyes through the masks we sometimes wear our own and others
- **Refusing** to let go of friendships with any unresolved hurt
- **Being** willing not to like or be liked by a friend during times of conflict

251.

- **Listening** WHEN WE FEEL LIKE TALKING, AND BELIEVING THAT FRIENDSHIPS ARE WORTH DOING THE EMOTIONAL WORK

MY WISH FOR ALL OF US IS TO RECOGNIZE THE ESSENTIAL VALUE OF OURSELVES AS A FRIEND, AND THE FRIENDS WE HAVE NOW AND HAVE HAD IN THE PAST.

I'd LIKE TO HONOR EACH OF MY ENDED OR INACTIVE FRIENDSHIPS WITH A HEARTY "THANK YOU" FOR WHAT WE SHARED AND ANY LESSONS LEARNED, AND A "PLEASE FORGIVE ME" FOR ANY WAYS I MAY HAVE CAUSED PAIN.

I'd LIKE TO ACKNOWLEDGE MY PRESENT FRIENDSHIPS WITH A LOVING SMILE AND A VERY FULL HEART. MY GRATITUDE TO EACH OF YOU.

I'M HAPPY TO THINK OF FRIENDS I HAVEN'T MET YET.

AS MY FRIEND ISABEL, WHO RECENTLY DIED IN HER 90'S SAID;

252.

"Your Friends Are your Gardens, and THAT includes the Weeds, snails and Full-Blown roses."

I HAVE A vision of All of our Friendship Gardens intersecting, Vines twining Together, Flowers in wild glee and All of our lAuGHTer Filling The Air.

I'll Be leArning Deeply, loving Wildly, and Living Fully with My Friends and invite YOU to Do The SAme.

Our collective Friendship energy is A power. full Good Force.

In Friendship and FAITH

love, Susan (SARK)

San Francisco
Summer 2006

253.

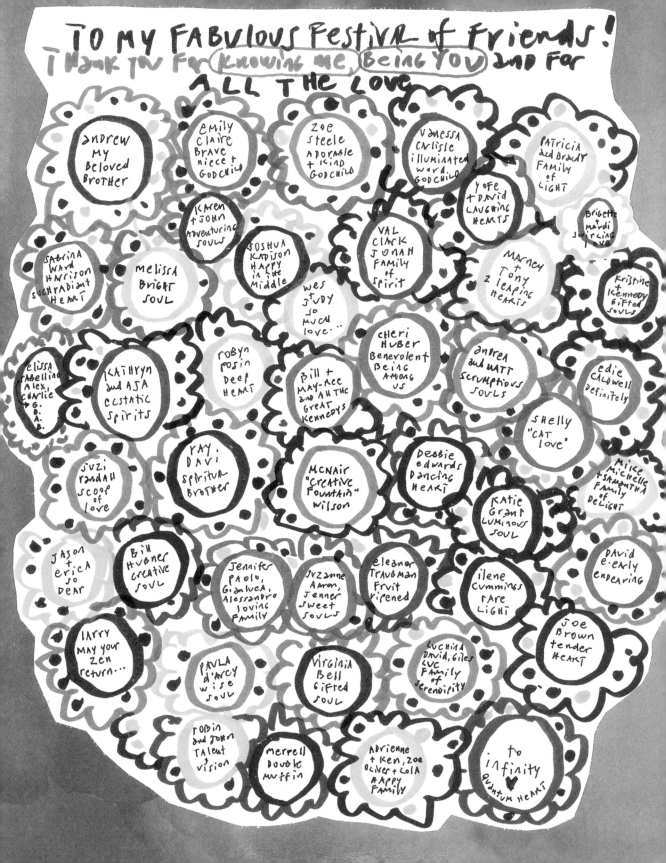

OTHER BOOKS BY SARK

VISIT ME AT
PLANET SARK.COM